concilium

1992/5

THE TABU OF DEMOCRACY WITHIN THE CHURCH

Edited by

James Provost and Knut Walf

SCM Press · London

October 1992

ISBN: 0 334 03016 1

Typeset at The Spartan Press Ltd, Lymington, Hants
Printed by Mackays of Chatham, Kent

Concilium: Published February, April, June, August, October, December

Contents

Editorial

The Tabu of Democracy within the Church

Surely, over past decades this theme has constantly been brought up, discussed, decided on in a more or less definitive way and then relegated to the archives – by some with resignation and by others with relief? Unless we are completely mistaken, the greatest common denominator in the results of reflections or even the fact on which all are agreed is ultimately that democratization is incompatible with the essence of the (Catholic) church. By that people mean that church and society are different, dissimilar entities, and that different parameters and structural forms apply to the internal formation of each.

Of course we have to begin with two terminological questions. First, what do we mean by 'democracy'? The term is determined sociologically, politically and by its particular cultural context.

Secondly, which Catholic church are we talking about? That in the West or that in the East (the so-called Uniate churches)? The church in the North Atlantic area or the church in the countries of Black Africa or Latin America? The church of former times or the church today? The church with its hierarchical structure or the orders?

There was and is 'democracy', or at least there were and are 'democratic' elements in the Catholic church, even in the 1983 Corpus of Canon Law (e.g. cc.127ff., 135ff., 208–23); further details can be found in the article by James Provost. Do we have to see a fatal positivism of tradition, as Peter Berger does, in the fact that under the influence of secular feudalistic forms of rule hierarchical structures have established themselves in the Catholic Church as well?

Here, then, we have a many-sided complex of questions with numerous aspects. Moreover, since we also have the efforts of very different academic disciplines with divergent theoretical approaches and methods, the results of the investigations were and are difficult to compare or to combine. The question of the democratization of the Catholic Church has been discussed constantly over the past thirty years, both inside and outside the church. Moreover, here and there attempts have been made to produce summaries of the various approaches and discussions. Consequently, we initially hesitated to discuss this many-facetted complex of questions within the comparatively narrow framework of the *Concilium* section on church order.

However, there is no mistaking the fact that there are two important reasons for a new treatment of the theme. First, in regions or states with lengthy democratic traditions there is some uncertainty, and sometimes even resignation, as to whether democracy of the traditional and indeed proven kind, parliamentary democracy, is the form of government best suited for coping with the gigantic problems of the present and the future. The incompetence of parliamentarians and democrats on substantive issues, corruption in political parties which can no longer be ignored, and many other factors, have contributed to bringing democracy into disrepute in the eyes of many citizens. Just one example of the way in which democratically legitimated institutions are often hardly still in a position to make important political decisions is the shift of decisions from the parliaments into the sphere of jurisprudence. This is a phenomenon which has recently been emerging in many democracies. Secondly, today a new fundamentalism is developing in the monotheistic religions which regards democratic elements within religion or the church as being completely alien to its nature. The existence of such constellations is yet another reason which makes further reflection on the subject worthwhile.

As early as the first preparations for this issue it became evident that the questions arising in this connection could hardly be discussed professionally by canon lawyers alone. As a rule the suggestions made by our colleagues for specific topics and competent authors went beyond the sphere of canon law.

So although we hear from some canon lawyers (B. Franck, P. Huizing, G. King, J. Provost), this issue contains contributions from other disciplines: by five theologians, two women (B. Klein Goldewijk and P. Walter) and three men (M. Legrain, G. Nedungatt, M. Volf); a political theorist (K. Tudyka); a historian (G. Alberigo); a doctor and psychologist who has also studied other disciplines (W. Obrist); and a theologian who is at the same time a sociologist (G. Baum).

James Provost
Knut Walf

Ecumenical Experiments in Ireland

We are daily confronted with the failure of institutions, both political or ecclesial, to deal effectively with intractable human problems, whether we look to Northern Ireland, the Middle East or Central Europe – just to mention three world flash-points that the writer of this column has recently experienced first hand. Sometimes, as in the case of Northern Ireland, the very situation for which remedy is now being sought is itself the product of those very institutions. Such is the tragic irony of our history.

Christians are people of hope. But where is hope to be found when the institutional upholders of our value systems seem incapable of relieving the real problems that afflict us? The answer must surely be in the responses of people working together in the power of the Spirit that transcends institutional boundaries. In theological terms such an understanding of the Spirit's uncontrolled and indefinable, yet real presence in our world is well documented in our foundational documents: 'The Spirit breathes where it wills' (John 3.8). This reassurance becomes a challenge to all of us when the boundaries that we establish for the very legitimate, even necessary reason of giving us some sense of self-identity, become a stumbling-block to growth and an obstacle to overcoming the antinomies that are involved in all self-definition, personal and communal.

In Northern Ireland today there are several such movements of the Spirit, movements that do not seek to ignore the institutional churches or their legitimate concerns, but which nevertheless are not restricted by the disciplines of these, as committed Christians from all the churches try to find a new road to reconciliation and peace based on their vision. In contrast with the daily catalogue of violence that we hear of in the media, these counter-cultural movements receive little public attention and their work might appear to be a drop in the ocean of despair. Yet many who are well acquainted with the problems that ordinary people face on a day-to-day basis are convinced that they represent a genuine development in the right direction. One sincerely hopes so. They have continued now for long enough to ensure that they are no mushroom growth, but are well grounded and thought-out strategies for confronting the religious factors that are such an integral part of the situation of conflict.

The Corrymeela Community was founded by concerned Christians from all the main churches in 1965, four years before the present wave of violence erupted. Today it has 150 formal members and over 1,000 friends scattered throughout the Northern Ireland community, but in other countries also, sharing in the Corrymeela vision of working for peace and reconciliation in their own local communities. That vision is very definitely evangelical, drawing on the memory of Jesus, who not only proclaimed a gospel of peace but also exposed those aspects of his own religious culture that were opposed to, or destructive of, God's universal plan. As a concrete expression of this radical vision those who visit Corrymeela have the opportunity to expose their lives to this radical critique within the context of a community life that seeks to give such a transforming vision around a small core group of residential volunteers. In such a setting people from all the churches or from none, and from across the class divide, act as resources to one another, drawing on their different life experiences and feeling free to expose these in an atmosphere of love and sharing. In such a setting even the potentially divisive experience of 'the Troubles' (as the conflict is often euphemistically called) can be discussed and its impact on the lives of the participants examined.

These groups are described in the best biblical tradition as 'seed groups', emphasising both the potentiality for growth and the risk factor involved in all forms of planting – particularly the risk of failure. Each group, comprising twenty people, meets for four week-ends, during which life experiences are explored and discussed through role-play, discussion and reflection in a supportive community atmosphere. On the final week-end the participants look to their future journeys, both individual and shared, and try to identify the directions they should take in the light of the encounter with one another and themselves in the context of Christian peace and healing.

Corrymeela is one of several such models to have emerged in Northern Ireland as a direct result of the social unrest and violence that has torn the community there apart for decades now. The Columbanus Community of peace and reconciliation is another with a rather different focus. Founded in 1983 by the Jesuit priest Father Michael Hurley, who had previously founded the highly successful Irish School of Ecumenics in Dublin, the Columbanus venture attempts to express Father Hurley's ecumenical vision within the troubled world of inner Belfast. It seeks to give a practical example of what a more united church, a more just society and a more peaceful world could be like. It is based on a community life of prayer and sharing in accordance with a common rule. The eucharist is celebrated together, but the members endure for the present the pain of not receiving communion in accordance with their denominational commitments. While the focus is decidedly on the community life the vision is outward looking, providing resources for various ecumenical agencies, especially promoting contact and co-operation between separated schools. While many see 'integrated schooling', that is children of all denominations attending the same school, as the solution to the problems of Northern Ireland, the Columbanus vision recognizes the impractical aspects of this proposal on a large scale and tries instead to foster good relations and understanding between the existing schools, that heretofore have operated in very separate worlds.

There are several other examples of new community initiatives in Northern Ireland today. These two – Corrymeela and Columbanus – have been chosen because they represent initiatives that might be said to be Protestant and Catholic, in that they have arisen from and to some extent reflect different emphases, emanating from different sides of the Christian dividing line. The one is word-centred, the other more sacramental, even monastic in inspiration. Yet neither is restricted by the past, but seeks to retrieve these very legitimate aspects of our common tradition in a challenging context that often borders on despair. Of such stuff is Christian hope made. Both are open to all dimensions of the common tradition. Both seek to remain in touch with, and be respectful of, the denominational expressions of that tradition that, acording to many, are part of the problem. They, and other such movements, are a summons to conversion to all the main churches. Whether they are cries that will go unheard in the wilderness, or sprouts of hope that are beginning to burst through the barren ground, depends on how open to the Spirit those institutions are. The Spirit breathes where it will.

Seán Freyne

I · Fundamental Questions

The Meaning of Democracy Today

Kurt Tudyka

The limits and possibilities of democracy have again become a topical theme. On the one hand the call for democracy accompanied the collapse of real socialism, the fall of dictatorships in the Third World and the constitution of new states. On the other hand it is confronted with the revival of pre-modern fundamentalist currents and the constant bureaucratic-technocratic transformation of society at the height of modernity. Democracy has changed, developed in different ways and spread in many forms, both in theory and in reality, between its Hellenistic origins and the twentieth century. So the term today has several meanings and refers to a variety of phenomena. This gives rise to many questions which are reappearing or are completely new.

This article sets out to deal with six questions which seem particularly important. First comes the theoretical question of the concept of democracy. Then comes the normative question of its basis. Thirdly, we need to ask what democracy consists of. An answer to this question involves not only a survey of the political geography of the global state system but also a sociological analysis of the politics of modern society. Here, then, are three spheres in which democracy functions, and each time the question arises how it functions in them, what the institutional and structural conditions for democracy are, how it copes with its internal contradictions and external dilemmas, restrictions and threats, and what are its possibilities and limits in each instance.

I. What is democracy?

Democracy essentially means rule of the people, in other words the sovereignty of the people: 'Rule of the people by the people for the people.' According to J. J. Rousseau, rulers and ruled are identical. All rule derives from the principle of the sovereignty of the people. The will of the people is equally binding on all citizens. Conversely, political decisions are only legitimate if they rest on the expression of the will of all citizens. Ideally these citizens form a homogenous society. Individual political actions do not have a quality of their own but are only the emanation of the one, inalienable sovereign power. Thus the subject-object relationships of traditional rule become an indivisible, permanent relationship between equal subjects with equal rights in the action and interaction of the government of their polity. According to a formulation of Rousseau's, democracy is 'a method of associating which will defend and collect, with all the collective might, the person and property of each associate and in virtue of which each associate, though he becomes a member of the group, nevertheless obeys only himself and remains as free as before'.[2] With his political involvement, the citizen who is of age is in a position to regulate the affairs of the polity along with all others. The general will is expressed in resolutions and laws, because the members of the society – thanks to its constitution released from particular interests – can recognize it and express it publicly. In the case of a vote the subjects have to acknowledge the majority decision for themselves as well; conversely, the majority has the task of acting for the totality.

Even Rousseau conceded that in reality the concept of democracy which he formulated never existed in a pure form and probably never would. In fact, democracy is in reality the constantly changing, provisional result of historical processes which consist of conflicts and compromises and which depend on social, economic and cultural developments. So in reality democracy is not just one particular form in which the will of the people is expressed. Democracy has appeared so far in a variety of forms and will continue to do so in the future. The following forms are distinct: direct, representative, committee, competitive and élitist democracy.

The form of direct democracy corresponds to the classic conception of democracy, according to which it not only serves as a means e.g. of recruiting a leadership among the members or of making decisions on general direction but also serves the aims of the members themselves, namely their individual personal development.

Representative democracy is the resolution of two kinds of conflict between the claim and the limitation of democracy. On the one hand it is an expedient for the direct democratic shaping of the will of a large number of members of a complex society, e.g. large territorial states or large organizations. Here it is presupposed that the individual interests of the subjects can be objectified, so that they can be determined by a leading group. On the other hand representative democracy departs from its justification, namely to make direct democracy possible under difficult conditions, when the representatives are regarded as a filter against the supposed dangers of an irrational shaping of the will of the people. If a gradated system of representation gives just as much contact with the population as necessary and puts as little limitation on the freedom of the leading group as possible, then the democratic legitimation becomes a hollow shell.

Committee democracy is the attempt at an alternative to an oligarchy clad in the form of representative democracy. Self-rule is not exercised regionally but functionally by a socially homogeneous group which strives for an identity between itself and its representatives: the greatest possible competence for the original electorate, the election of the occupants of all leading positions, an imperative mandate on the representatives, accountability and the possibility of dismissal, honorary office or only minimal financial remuneration for officials. If the realization of this model does not become an alternative to the representation model, then as an expansion of it it at least represents a heightened democratization of society.

Competitive democracy or élitist democracy is a departure from ideas of direct democracy. The competition between the leading groups, parties or associations is simply to make possible the selection of a leadership. This model is a distortion of the classical notion of democracy. In view of the specialization and differentiation of modern societies its supporters regard it as the only possible form of democracy, as 'realistic democracy'. According to J. Schumpeter, the citizens also have to respect the division of work between themselves and the politicians which they have elected: 'They may not all too readily withdraw their trust in politicians between elections and must see that once they have chosen someone, political activity is his concern and not theirs.'[3] The electorate are regarded as consumers in a market of offers, which are made by the political élite to assert their position.

II. Why democracy?

Democracy can be justified in a variety of ways: anthropologically, by legitimation; pragmatically, in terms of achievement and system theory.

At the centre of the anthropological justification stands value as something which is indispensable for all human beings. It comes about through the possibility of the free development of the person who has come of age, and only a democratic polity offers the conditions for it. Democracy is a form of human self-realization.

Democracy can be justified by legitimation on the basis of pre-existing human rights from which democracy is derived and to which it also remains tied. Such a reciprocal connection also justifies democracy in the name of human rights: only through democracy are human rights implemented. Finally, elements of democracy are themselves seen as a part of human rights, like freedom of thought, opinion, assembly and association.

Pragmatic reasons for democracy are its suitability for the limitation, mitigation or even resolution of conflicts and the basis for peace and training towards a readiness for peace which results from this. There is also empirical evidence that states with a democratic constitution always prefer compromise to war in cases where interests differ.

Justification of democracy in terms of achievement points to the motivation, stimulation and creative forces which are released both by active participation in decisions and also by competitive behaviour. Democratic processes lead to better solutions than hierarchical decisions. Democracy is to be preferred to other forms of rule because in the long run its system causes the least friction or cost.

System theory regards democracy as a means of providing inner stabilization for systems. It develops communicative relationships which tend to contribute towards an equilibrium in the system. This is expressed in concrete terms in their contribution towards social justice and thus social balance.

III. What does democracy consist of?

The question of the place and dissemination of democracy has first to be answered in terms of political geography and then in terms of political sociology.

After the Second World War democracy established itself all over the world as a norm in all states – though with considerable differences in interpretation and therefore in different ways. Nowadays, in contrast to the first half of the twentieth century, no political system, nor even any political movement worth mentioning, identifies itself explicitly with anti-democratic values. Democracy is claimed universally, at least as a label. It has become an evolutionary universal.

Necessary and important principles, institutions and procedures belonging to democracy have become codified by international law as ingredients of human rights, for example by the passing of the Universal Declaration on Human Rights at the UN General Assembly in 1948 and by the 1966 international pact on civil and political rights which more than ninety states have ratified since then. These guarantee above all rights to freedom of expression and freedom of association and assembly. Article 21 of the Universal Declaration of Human Rights also grants everyone the right to take part in the shaping of the public affairs of his or her country, directly, or through freely elected representatives, and to have access to public offices on the same conditions. The last section of the article even states that the will of the people is the basis of the authority of government. It further states that this will shall be expressed in periodic and genuine elections which shall be by universal and equal suffrage and shall be held by secret vote or equivalent free voting procedures.

States acknowledge similar largely democratic principles through regional agreements, like the 1950 European Convention on the Protection of Human Rights and Basic Freedoms and the 1982 Pan-African Banjul Charter of Human Rights and the Rights of Peoples. All the European and North American states have come furthest in also acknowledging democratic principles internationally in the Charter of the Conference for Security and Collaboration in Europe which was drawn up in Paris in 1990.

However, all over the world the understanding and practice of democracy differ widely. In many countries there is not only a lack of institutional conditions, but even of cognitive, social and economic conditions for an adequate acceptance, capacity and readiness for the formation of a democratic will, the making of democratic decisions and the implementation of the decisions.

In this connection problems arise which democracy cannot solve. Internal contradictions and external dilemmas emerge. On the one hand democracy as a norm serves to legitimate rulers in the exercising of their power. On the other hand it is claimed as a legitimation for the activity of those who oppose this exercise of power or even the whole form of rule. In extreme cases this activity which takes place on the pretext of democracy can aim at its limitation or – as in the 1920s in Europe – even its abolition. So in being made concrete, democracy needs a minimum of unviolable basic rules recognized by all those involved in it. The question remains what is to be done with those who deliberately seek to violate these rules, e.g. some un- or anti-democratic groups which nevertheless appeal to democratic rights for their activity as long as they have not gained power.

Another problem is the fragmentation of a society into a variety of closed, culturally homogeneous groups, whether through race, religion, language or whatever. The identification and acknowledgment of their position by the granting of special rights, like *a priori* quotas of seats on committees and boards, in parliament and government, limit the democratic rights of emancipated individuals. In such circumstances, minority rights violate democracy. For instead of gaining a majority of votes in the process of the formation of a democratic opinion, individuals are reminded of or even obligated to their membership of their group. On the other hand, if the quantitative predominance of a homogenous group, e.g. an ethnic group, constantly leads to the outvoting of another, the group outvoted will again indicate its loyalty to such a polity. The demand for the self-determination of peoples thus develops out of opposition to the practice of democracy.

The legal acknowledgment and existence of principles, institutions and procedures as the necessary elements of democracy is therefore not enough. Democracy must also be lived out, and that calls for a corresponding political culture. The political reality of many countries is remote from that. This reality is full of distortions which already betray their nature by their nomenclature, like 'popular democracy' or 'guided democracy'.

Democracy has no clear and irreversible place in modern society. We can distinguish roughly three areas to which democracy extends at present, conceptually and in practice. These are democracy as a political system, democracy as internal organization and democracy as a living culture.

The traditional conceptions of democracy are directed exclusively or at any rate primarily towards the formation of the state. The forms, agents, processes and rules and the legitimation of the system of government – different though they were – were the objects of the attention of those who thought about good polity in the ancient polis (Plato and Aristotle); the political philosophers of the Enlightenment (Rousseau and Montesquieu) and the constitutional theorists from the eighteenth century on (Hamilton, Jefferson, John Stuart Mill, Tocqueville).

Despite the long practice of internal democracy in traditional communities, like orders, guilds and cathedral chapters, systematic consideration and reflection on a democracy which also applied to non-state organization only developed among sociologists and political theorists (Michels) with the rise of highly complex and differentiated societies from the beginning of the twentieth century on.

Democracy as the expression of a particular political culture and its ideas of value as behaviour to be learned in a historical process only found the attention it deserved, going beyond sporadic statements, in the twentieth century (Almond, Verba).

Since the eighteenth century democracy has not only come to be established as a system of government but has also become the dominant principle of legitimation, order and conduct. Democracy is the form in which modernity is shaped.

IV. Democracy as a system of government

Democracy originally meant only the state form of rule and, in the narrower sense, even only legislation on a simple matter. The term 'people' was also defined narrowly. According to the idea of the equality of individuals as the presupposition for democratic rights, this should pertain only to propertied citizens.

In the twentieth century views about the subjects and objects of the democratic exercise of rule have changed. First, those who take part in democratic processes have been put on an equal footing legally and their categories have been extended (e.g. by the abolition of privileges of state or class and the right to plural votes, the rule of one person one vote, and the introduction of universal suffrage, including women and younger age-groups). Secondly, all public affairs have gradually come to be subjected, albeit often indirectly and with checks and balances, to democratic legitimation.

In the meantime the concept of democracy has also come to be understood as competitive democracy in the sense of the competition of collective organizations which transcend individuals. Here people talk of party democracy in the case of parties and of pluralist democracy in the case of groups. The claim to direct decisions by citizens has remained alongside this in the form of plebiscitary democracy by means of referenda, petitions and plebiscites. The concept of economic democracy, which seeks to involve representatives of the workers in economic and economic-political decisions at all levels, is a mixture of direct and indirect components of democracy.

In theory and in practice democracy has been bound up with a series of necessary and additional principles, institutions and procedures. They derive primarily from a liberal tradition of thought and practice. Democratic and liberal components have combined in a dialectical way: on the one hand freedom presupposes equality, but on the other striving for equality must not threaten freedom.

A first element of democracy is the possibility of articulating the political will. Here the fundamental presupposition is that consensus can be achieved. If there is no possibility of a complete consensus, then the right to elect and vote becomes the presupposition for the formation of a democratic will. Here the majority principle is recognized as a criterion for decision. Finally implementation in accordance with the decision concludes the core of the democratic process.

However, according to prevailing ideas and practices the presuppositions mentioned are not enough to justify unconditionally giving the predicate democratic to a process of forming a will and a decision. So additional conditions are freedom to articulate the will publicly and with equal rights (freedom of opinion, speech, the press, assembly, demonstration and association), the active and passive right to vote, secret elections and voting and public information about the result and its implementation, and legal protection for subject minorities.

Depending on the specific circumstances, there is a further number of formal and material conditions which can guarantee the observation of the presuppositions mentioned, e.g. adequate information about and access to the places or times for elections and votes, terms laid down for offices and decisions, government for a period, more candidates than offices, alternative proposals for elections and votes, the rotation of offices, the possibility of dismissal from office. Finally, to avoid the false development and misuse of the democratic process and to optimize it, some institutions which by nature cannot be done away with are necessary frameworks. These include human rights, the legal state and independent jurisdiction which also covers matters relating to the political constitution.

Democracy came to full fruition only through a further division and separation of state authority in the form of the separation of legislation from the implementation of the law and through federalism with the principle of subsidiarity. In the course of the concretizing of democracy, further questions arise which stress more the character of democracy as a goal or a means, like grass-roots or representative democracy, the right to proportional representation or majority vote, preliminary elections, preliminary votes, referenda or the election of representatives.

Over against the power of the executives and the administration, which has increased in the modern state, new forms of democratic influence by citizens have developed in the implementation of politics. These include hearings, objections and complaints against the plans and decisions of the administration like appeals to the Ombudsman in the case of defective administrative procedures. One effect of the desire for sustainable environmental conditions is the participation of the public, and above all citizens who are affected, in the planning process for major projects which have an effect on the environment like dams, airports, motorways, or nuclear installations before consent is given for their construction.

Such rights have only arisen not least through the protest of those directly involved, which is expressed in many ways, for example through local meetings, the blocking of streets, demonstrations aimed at media coverage (in the style of Greenpeace), sit-ins or go-ins and a refusal to pay taxes to the state. Such protests have been organized by civil initiatives and action committees. What they have in common, and what distinguishes them from parties, is their limited duration and their orientation on a particular problem.

At the end of the twentieth century democracy seems to be being impaired in three ways. First, a hierarchical rule of élites which in part still has a premodern basis is asserting itself through self-recruitment. On the other hand a late-modern, specialized bureaucratic and technocratic rule has developed, bound up with functional efficiency. Parallel to this, the political system is shifting from its democratic basis, in that democracy is functioning less and less as the transmission of expressions of the will of the people. Instead of this it is reduced to the selection and legitimation of a political class ('political élite') which as the representative of the people is only mediating its interests ('élite democracy'). Finally, thirdly, there is a threat that democracy will lose mass loyalty under conditions of social and economic decline, because it seems caught up in a vicious triangle of rising expectations of prosperity, the capacity of the state for action and the autonomy of business. In this connection the material support of societies which are 'being transformed' into democracies, which is generally thought necessary, is ambivalent. For whereas democracy was formerly an expression of a desire of the underprivileged, it now appears as a mechanism of political guidance which has to be shielded and protected against disruption or even attack by the failure of the economic system. The more democracy as a system of government is overburdened with expectations of prosperity which cannot be met, the less it may limit itself to the institutional order of the state and its leadership if its values are to be preserved.

V. Democracy as internal organization

Democracy has been transferred to spheres outside the state. Here the practice of state democracy has provided models both for the possibilities and for the limits of participation by the members of non-state organizations, of associations and groups. The principle of democracy is claimed for different social, cultural and above all economic spheres ('industrial democracy') by the demand for internal democratization ('participatory democracy') for both public bodies and institutions and private organizations (e.g. in social welfare, training and educational institutions, in universities, the administration, in businesses, in parties, associations and unions).

There are extra-organizational and intra-organizational reasons for the democratization of organizations. If democracy is not to wither away and become something practised now and then in leisure time or at festivals, it must be practised permanently as participation or involvement in the sphere of work, everyday life and leisure. No authoritarian spheres should be able to exist side by side with mere democratic islands in a society.

Since particularly in the circumstances of pluralistic democracy the leadership of the groups, associations and organizations involved in it can occupy an oligarchical position in relation to their organized members, the demand follows for an internal democratization of these groups themselves.

Finally, empirical studies also indicate that among the members of an organization the motivation for activity and identification with the organization increases on the basis of inner democratization. This brings about an increase not only in their efficiency and productivity but also in the creativity and flexibility of the organization's strategy in competition with others.

In analogy to the state sphere, there are different forms of organizational democratization, such as direct, representative or committee democracy. The latter above all has spread through the framework of public life, professional life and the world of work by parents' committees, social welfare committees, university committees, radio and television committees, business committees and administrative committees.

On the basis of such developments and above all their own claims, those employed in business enterprises, in factories and in administration have won the right to speak and vote in different forms and to different extents. Even the army requires not only the citizen to have rights in uniform, i.e. the right of soldiers to vote and take part in the political system, but also the professional representation of soldiers' interests, e.g. through trade union organization or the representation of their interests in their sphere of activity as internal democratization through personnel committees.

However, organizations which are becoming increasingly complex require appropriate forms of participation if they are not to exhaust democracy and democratization in the sham of pseudo-democratic rituals.

VI. Democracy as political culture

The consequence is that if it is to have substance, democracy cannot be thought of and practised statutorily and with instrumental limitations as a means of gaining power. Rather, democracy gains permanence only as a developing process which takes note of the participation of men and women in connection with the changes in the modern world.

Democracy must be so rooted in the perceptions, feelings and values of the members of society that they are also ready to take part in public life and not react apathetically, withdrawing into private niches. Democracy will find it difficult to develop where society is dominated or imposed on by personality structures like subject mentality, opportunism or the 'authoritarian personality'. A democratic political culture consists of beliefs, attitudes and values which point the members of the society towards participation in democratic institutions and procedures.

Democracy can only develop when the introduction of institutional and procedural forms goes hand in hand with a break in or at least a change of values in a society which is transforming itself into a democracy.

Translated by John Bowden

Bibliography

R. Dahl, *Democracy and its Critics*, New Haven and London 1989

A. Downs, *Ökonomische Theorie der Demokratie*, Tübingen 1968

M. Etzioni-Halevy, *Bureaucracy and Democracy: A Political Dilemma*, London 1983

F. Gloede (ed.), *Öffentlichkeitsbeteilung – politisches Forum oder notwendiges Übel?*, Frankfurt am Main 1992

J. Habermas, 'Reflexionen über den Begriff der politischen Beteiligung', in Habermas et al., *Student und Politik*, Neuwied 1961

H. S. Kariel (ed.), *Frontiers of Democratic Theory*, New York 1970

G. Leibolz, *Strukturproblem der modernen Demokratie*, Karslruhe ²1968

R. Michels, *Zur Sociologie des Parteiwesens in der modernen Demokratie* (1925), Stuttgart 1957

J. S. Mill, *Representative Government* (1861), Oxford 1975

F. Naschold, *Organisation und Demokratie*, Stuttgart 1969

C. Pateman, *Participation and Democratic Theory*, Cambridge 1970

G. Sartori, *The Theory of Democracy Revisited*. Chatham 1987

J. A. Schumpeter, *Capitalism, Socialism and Democracy*, New York 1942

Notes

1. Abraham Lincoln, Gettysburg 1863.
2. J. J. Rousseau, *The Social Contract*, Gateway Edition 1954, 18.
3. J. A. Schumpeter, *Capitalism, Socialism and Democracy*, New York 1942.

Ecclesiology and Democracy: Convergences and Divergences

Giuseppe Alberigo

Christianity, the church and democracy have a history extending over centuries, even millennia, even if they have only come together very recently. The church has had no difficulty in presenting itself as a monarchy (only then to enter into rivalry with the monarchies), has reflected the hierarchical structure of feudal society, and has joined forces with the communes, the upper classes and with absolutism. However, the relationship with democracy has been difficult: for a long time there has been conflict, and only over recent decades has there been a cautious rapprochement. The sacral exterior of the monarchy and of feudalism, both of which formally respected the divine origin of power, were no part of democracy, which postulates a human origin for authority. Moreover, in the eyes of Catholicism, the 'lay' and 'secular' character of democracy was heightened by its original dissemination in areas with a Protestant majority or a Gallican tradition. Finally, the progressive prevalence of the 'universalist' conception of the church has made a reference to the monarchy seem more apt, the democratic order being homogeneous with the view of the church as a communion of local communities. These are the profound reasons for the mistrust of this political system by the church, a hostility only overcome a century ago and only in the social order, not within the internal government of the church.[1]

However, we cannot ignore the many points of contact which exist, at both a doctrinal and a practical level, between central aspects of Christianity and the fundamental aspects of democracy. The electoral method has always been part of the Christian community – albeit with varying fortunes;[2] the principle *quod omnes tangit, ab omnibus tractari et approbari debet*, that all ought to be involved in matters which concern everyone, combined with the majoritarian criterion, was one of the cardinal points of mediaeval ecclesiology;[3] a major council solemnly elaborated the dynamic relationship between the divine origin of authority in the church and the sovereignty of the *universitas fidelium*.[4]

Again, the fact that the pope is elected and the indefectibility of the *sensus fidei*[5] of the community of believers are now characteristic elements of the institutional structure and of Catholic dogmatics. Last of all, John Paul II has based his pontificate on the promotion of human rights, thus bringing about a new convergence between Catholicism and democracy.

So is a democratization of the church possible? Is it at least possible to hypothesize an introduction of the democratic method into the church?[6]

Democracy in the church?

Any reply has to be largely empirical. In fact on the one hand 'democracy' in contemporary cultures has differing meanings; what we see is not so much a single system, far less a *Weltanschauung*, but rather a group of methods for regulating political life which command a consensus above all in the societies of the northern hemisphere of the planet. On the other hand, it has been clearly recognized that the Christian church is in origin a 'convocation' regulated by the covenant between God and human beings, 'from Abel to the last of the righteous'. Here is a metahistorical element – a call responded to by a faith – which makes the church unique, at the institutional level as well. Every time that a political model is applied too mechanically to the Christian church there is the risk of polluting, destroying or changing this basic nucleus of its nature.

In the various historical cycles so far it has been the experience of the church that it constitutes a 'model' for political societies, though sometimes the opposite has proved the case (and today a number of people are in fact asking whether the church should not adapt itself to the democratic model). However, the most fruitful elements of this relationship have always been characterized by indirect transpositions and analogies, whether from the church to society or vice versa.

Up to the beginning of this century, structurally the Catholic church appeared to be organized according to a pyramidal scheme, the result of a sedimentation extending over many centuries, emphasized in more recent decades by an accelerated radicalization. The ecclesiastical pyramid seemed to be headed by the pope, who was the apex and the source of legitimation. Then came the bishops – often seen as representatives of the pope in the various provinces of the church (dioceses); with the pope they formed the 'ecclesiastical hierarchy'. Further down the pyramid came the clergy – both the secular clergy and those in orders – and the mass of the faithful. These formed the massive base of the pyramid and were the principal and essentially passive recipients of the activity, decisions and teaching of the authorities (sacraments, preaching, internal discipline, ethical behaviour).[7]

The ecclesiastical pyramid had been given a doctrinal dimension which put the emphasis above all on the pope and his faithful.[8] The pope was presented as the 'vicar of Christ', endowed with singular powers and privileges not shared with others (*plenitudo potestatis*). All other authority in the church derived from him, and he was the sole source of it; the bishops themselves, even when solemnly gathered in council, did not have any other authority than that attributed to them by the pope. Alongside the ecclesiastical pole, the faithful formed the second firm pole of the church, but had an essentially passive role (the 'learning' church), and only small qualified groups (Catholic Action) were accepted for work – as sub-ordinates – with the ecclesiastical class. The ordinary faithful *qua* laity (i.e. not as members of the clergy) were in a condition of subjection, with no positive connotations nor any significant way of expressing themselves, so that it could be said that the whole Catholic church was one great parish of universal dimensions of which the pope was the parish priest. In this context the hypothesis of a relationship between the church and democracy appeared subversive.[9]

Today the problems in this relationship have been eased by the way in which Vatican II has developed the aspect of the church as communion (*koinonia*), brought into being by the Spirit and structured by the sacraments, above all baptism. According to this ecclesiology,[10] the church is the people of God travelling in history between the incarnation and the second coming of Christ. These constitutive and immutable data, in due course referred to as *status ecclesiae*,[11] divine law,[12] the essence of Christianity, are relatively circumscribed and have not prevented the church or its parts in the course of their historical experience from adopting very different institutional forms (*statuta ecclesiae*), depending on the impulse of the Spirit or cultural circumstances.

The people of God – 'a chosen race, a royal priesthood, a holy nation' (I Peter 2. 9) – and each of its members participate in the prophetic, kingly and priestly qualities of Christ himself.[13] That makes all the faithful equal, apart from the different measure of the faith of each one of them, and it equips all for the many services necessary for the life of the ecclesial community. Further sacramental sanctions (holy orders, episcopal consecration, marriage) ratify and specify the diversity of destinations and responsibilities.[14]

This substantial and original equality is the basis for the choice of persons to exercise ecclesial or electoral responsibilities (deacons, priests, bishops, etc.). That has been the case for a long time and can be the case again on the basis of electoral procedures in the democratic usage of this word, i.e. with the participation of all. The democratic sense of 'election' moreover fits well with its 'theological' meaning, implying divine calling guaranteed and expressed in the sacrament.[15] The democratic method could also be followed for appointments to service or responsibility for whole ecclesial communities, and not just individuals.

The use of the democratic method in the church not only as a determination which respects the majority but also as a habitual involvement of the *universitas fidelium* can affect many aspects of church structure in a variety of ways.

Services in the church and the democratic method

The sacrament of baptism makes any individual a member of the church by incorporating them fully into what is essentially a social reality, albeit one which is *sui generis*. This is a reality which from the New Testament onwards is called the 'body of Christ' or people of God, emphasizing the communal nature of Christianity. Christianity has never been a matter of an individual act but a sharing, communion. Such a characteristic puts the Christian church in a historical perspective which converges with many aspects of democracy, in so far as democracy is a set of rules aimed at allowing a number of subjects who are equal under the law to live together in society.

If they are reconsidered from this perspective, the fundamental dimensions of the life of the church fit in with and back up this convergence.

The liturgy as the characteristic act of the people of God is the act of many people, which by its very nature needs to be structured in such a way as to require the active involvement of all (*actuosa participatio*, as Vatican II puts it), though in different and complementary ways. Each time that this basic requirement is neglected, the church itself is disfigured and the liturgical act becomes fossilized, losing its clarity as a testimony to communion with the Father of the ecclesial communities and among the faithful themselves and therefore potentially with all humanity. The exclusion of the people of the faithful from the creativity of celebrations, which has now happened in the name of the 'purity' and 'regularity' of the rites, imposing a uniform culture from on high, has had the effect of marginalizing popular piety, but also of evacuating the liturgy, giving place to a division between official 'rituality' and popular 'devotions'.[16] In different historical periods the confraternities and the movements have often been the reaction to this expropriation of the faithful.

In this context also belong the problems relating to the recognition of the exemplary nature of the life of some Christians, the 'saints'. The preoccupation with guaranteeing the correctness of such recognition has led to the formulation of complex procedures of 'canonization', which have removed responsibility from the Christian community, relegating it to a passive position which is exclusively that of the 'consumer'. It is well known what distortions arise from this at the doctrinal level as well, to the degree that for centuries what has been recognized has been almost exclusively a sanctity of the highest classes (sovereigns, 'lords', etc.) or at any rate one that is alien to the condition of ordinary Christians (in that it comprises only popes, bishops, priests and brethren, monarchs, etc.).[17]

Paradoxically, one of the arguments used most frequently in favour of these expropriations lies in the affirmation that in this way the faithful are defended from the abuses of particular groups, since otherwise they would be deceived and exploited. This is an argument which is always used when there is a desire to impose a discipline from on high, without popular participation or consent. All attacks on democratic regimes tend to have something of this kind about them, going so far as the burning of 'dangerous' books (and even persons). This has an undercurrent which is not only politically unacceptable because it denies the capacity for discernment of the ordinary citizen, but is also aberrant from the ecclesiological point of view because it at least implies the rejection of the *sensus fidei* of the community.

The *sensus fidei* of the people of God in all its complexity above all constitutes a crucial link which has still not been analysed sufficiently, particularly in connection with the emphasis put on the *magisterium*.[18] In ecclesial physiology it is the *sensus fidei* above all which plays a decisive and creative role, whereas the *magisterium* has to be limited to the responsibility for authentication, for confirmation in the faith. The profession lived out in faith by some of the faithful, their orthopraxis which constitutes the 'concrete catechism', is the constant and irreplaceable testimony to and representation of the gospel for all humanity. In more recent centuries the scope of the *sensus fidelium* has been increasingly circumscribed, to the point that it has almost become an abstraction. Too many people accept its importance only in terms of 'reception',[19] i.e. of consent which is given after the event (and often passively, as a matter of duty) to conclusions arrived at previously by the authorities. The scholastic model of bourgeois society, entirely dominated by an exclusively 'descending' sense, has profoundly influenced this tendency to reverse the roles between the *sensus fidelium* and the *magisterium*. It is significant that these forms prove to be alien above all to less educated cultures.

At this level we find one of the most tenacious instances of resistance to the ecclesial use of aspects of the democratic method. It is countered that determining whether something is in conformity with revelation cannot be entrusted to the dialectic between majority and minority. But it should be noted that on the one hand this is a classical argument used in resisting democracy and, above all, on the other that it ignores the ineradicable qualitative difference between the church and civil society in that the *sensus fidelium* is rooted in the faith and is strengthened by the inspiration of the Spirit.[20] If this were not the case, how would the great Christian tradition have been able to accept the approval of the majority in conciliar decisions, from that of the Council of Jerusalem (Acts 15.1–29) onwards? It is correct, but also too easy, to stress the difficulties inherent in the criteria for accepting the consensus of the majority; it remains true that on the historical occasions on which it has been necessary, the discernment of the church has been effective. This does not mean abandoning oneself to providentialism, but affirming the conviction that the problem is not insoluble, as the past itself shows.

Alongside the *munera* of sanctification and testimony (*munus sacerdotale*) and of teaching/profession of the faith (*munus profeticum*), Christian ecclesiology has traditionally recognized a *munus regale*, which is expressed in service and responsibility for the leadership of the community. Here references to the democratic method are increasingly evident, and also less mechanical. In fact, the formation of basic choices and control of the implementation of the choices is one of the most intractable and controversial aspects in any democratic regime. Even Vatican II did not get beyond some theoretical assertions when it tried to make statements in this connection, and did not succeed in giving any specific guidelines.

The key issue of synodicality

The fundamental criterion is that of synodicality, which significantly is shared by all the great Christian traditions, though with different emphases and at different stages.[21] This criterion was taken up by Vatican II, both in the very holding of the council and in the ecclesiological pointers which prevailed at it; in turn the World Council of Churches has adopted the criterion with deep commitment.[22] Here too the analogy with a fundamental dimension of democracy is evident, though this should not lead us to ignore the limits and the contradictions which the method of holding assemblies has thrown up in almost all democratic experience. At a general level, as is already beginning to happen – albeit very timidly with the Synod of Bishops and with some consistories dedicated to specific matters – it will be important for there to be experiences of effective co-responsibility in shaping major and complex orientations, avoiding the temptation to be content with formal and ultimately triumphalistic choruses. The local experiments which are going on – at a continental, national, regional and diocesan level – of holding synods to achieve an increasingly wide involvement that can help the whole community to profit from the riches of the diversity of charisms are equally important.[23]

The growing imbalance between the number of priests and the number of territorial communities seems to be an urgent indication of the need for more elastic forms of ministry and availability than those which were tried out in past centuries through the presidency of Christian communities (which were essentially 'monarchical' or 'lordly'). In the long term it will be above all at this basic level that it will be possible to bring about a reappropriation of effective co-responsibility. It is here that the Christian community can also acquire and consolidate the habit of transparency, from the economic sphere to that of reading the signs of the time. 'Give a reason for the faith which is in us' (I Peter 3.15) is not an impalpable spiritual authority but a specific commitment from which no one is exempt and which is above all binding on those in positions of responsibility. Above all within modern Roman Catholicism people have become used to control being exercised from above (whether they exercise it or contest it), whereas in a healthy ecclesiology of communion the control has to be 'circular', as is implied by the ancient practice of *correctio fraterna*, which is structurally reciprocal.

So the perception which is widespread in so many Christian spheres of the parallelisms and convergences between Christianity and democracy is not a forced one, even if the central Roman authorities are showing doctrinal mistrust and active resistance. However, the sphere and the limits of these relationships need to be made more precise, particularly if they are to be translated into modifications of mentalities and structures.

The point of maximum contact, which is also that of most marked divergence, is over the equivalence of all Christians in the church to that of all members within a democratic society.[24] In fact, while it is undeniable that baptism constitutes a person a member of the ecclesial community with an even greater radicalism and definiteness than the effects of the attribution of citizenship in a democratic state, on the other hand it is clear that whereas in democracy the people is the prime holder and ultimate repository of power, in the church the sources of all responsibility and all mandates to service lie in Christ, and that these can be participated in only by means of a sacramental act.

On that basis it would not make sense to affirm that 'the church is a democracy', just as it never made sense to argue that 'the church is a monarchy' or 'the church is an aristocracy'.

However, the introduction into the church of aspects of the democratic method is a different matter. In truth, in this connection Christians are in the presence of a characteristic 'sign of the time', constituted by the request for participation and co-responsibility which characterizes the majority of contemporary cultures.[25] In fact this demand, so often made by groups which are economically and culturally marginalized, clearly bears the hallmark of the gospel in that it leads us to rediscover important aspects of the primitive Christian proclamation which successive centuries have disguised, and have even banished them to the world of utopias. The brotherhood which makes all – both individual Christians and individual churches – equal in dignity and in responsibility, the complementarity of the charisms which form the precious and inalienable treasure of each community, the chorality in the important actions of each church, are widespread and constant characteristics in primitive Christianity, despite their rugged diversity.

That is important, not as sustenance for an erudite or nostalgic archaeologism, but because it bears cogent testimony to an origin which, over and above practices adopted spontaneously in very diverse spheres (Jewish, Hellenistic, Roman, Persian, etc.), indicates an inspiration that goes back to the apostolic community and to Jesus' own preaching.

In the light of this, there is no question of schematically coming down in favour of a complete identity (or division) between democracy and Christianity. Rather, we must understand how the democratic authority demanded by Christians is a richer and fuller development of features of the gospel which have been obscured for too long. There are important and significant analogies between Christianity and democracy, the full scope of which is not always perceived, and which deserve further investigation and development.

Analogical relations

The relationship between Christianity and democracy is not an ontological and static given, but depends on historical and cultural contexts which are by definition changeable. It therefore involves analogies which have to be rethought and sometimes put in different social situations, as for example those which at present characterize the northern and southern hemispheres of our planet respectively. In any situation these analogies are partial and necessarily approximate. If, for example, it is quite evident that democracy implies and nourishes a social dynamism of individual and groups, in turn the centrality in Christianity of the trinitarian reference generates an ecclesial dynamism which is not only expressed in the inner universe of the believer or in the metahistorical mystery of the communion of saints but can and should also manifest itself in the historical order of the church.[26]

From it derives the legitimacy of creating situations, occasions and institutions which allow and favour – or at least do not get in the way of – the expressions of such dynamism. There is a vital need for dynamism between laity and clergy, between women and men, between uneducated and educated; also between committed communities at one of the poles of the gospel (word, charity, mission, prayer, eucharist); and finally, between small communities, historical traditions (Roman Catholic, Orthodox, Anglican, Protestant) and the great church. Outside this dynamic it is impossible, or a matter of sheer nominalism, to understand the Christian church as communion – far less as the people of God.

It seems to me that in this case an analogy can be recognized between ecclesial dynamism and democratic dynamism, though we must also be aware that the original trinitarian dynamism is much more radical and much more complex than that of the democratic matrix. In the present state of the life of the church why not recognize that the dynamism of democracy can offer valid stimuli and points of references for extending ecclesial dynamism and making it more effective (rather than evanescent and abstract)?

The analogy between democracy and Christianity is a very different one when it comes to guarantees. The democratic regimes entrust the guarantee that social rules will be respected first of all to a constitutional pact and secondarily to a distinction between powers. Recently, attempts have been made in the Catholic church to adopt the same course with the formulation in the 1960s of a project of 'fundamental law' (*Lex Ecclesiae fundamentalis*). The confrontation which developed as a result brought out the impracticability of this. Opposition came essentially in the name of the profound nature of the church which, unlike democratic regimes, does not have its own foundation in itself (and moreover, in the latter the authority of the constitutions is diminishing). It has to be seen that the guarantees of the ecclesial communion, while being no less important than those needed in democratic systems, are essentially rooted in the conscience of the *universitas fidelium* with modest and partial institutional projections.[27]

Similar considerations relate to the significance of the principle of subsidiarity, according to which the more complex authorities can only take over the responsibilities of the basic social realities in emergencies or as a supplement to them. In fact this principle has an important function in the social and political sphere, given that in democratic orders the point of reference is the state. However, in the church the real point of reference is above all the eucharistic community, i.e. the local church, and not just the universal church. Moreover, the eucharistic community is an essential factor in Christian ecclesiology, and therefore an abuse of subsidiarity on the part of the wider authorities is not only a functional *vulnus*, a wound, but also disrupts the fundamental economy of the church.[28]

So the relations between Christianity and democracy are effective and significant, provided that it is recognized that they are both analogical and imperfect. To reject a naive mechanical concealment of the structures of the church on the basis of the democratic method also guarantees that the church will not run the risk of repeating in our age the experience of the form of Christianity ('Christendom') which conditioned and burdened much of the mediaeval period. If in fact Christendom is seen as the name for a relationship of tendentious and reciprocal identification and reciprocal support between society and church, we must remember that today a parallelism between the democratic system and ecclesial regimes could produce equivalent effects. That would imprison the church in a historical and transitory system and prevent it from discharging a function of criticism and stimulus in the face of social systems. At all events, the most authentic support that the church can give to a democratic order of society remains that of an effective and increasingly profound praxis of communion within itself.

The older Christian tradition identifies, characterizes and describes the church in terms of the notes of unity, holiness, catholicity and apostolicity. That is also important in connection with 'democratization'. The church is not a formless entity which can be shaped in unlimited ways; its essential physiognomy is a given. The 'notes' express it adequately, above all in their circularity and complementarity. The analogy with democracy cannot ignore them, far less harm damage them.

Can the dynamic consonance between the *lex orandi* and the *lex credendi* express creatively and in a coherent way a *lex communionis*, that is, rules and institutions, and above all a style and a mentality suitable for serving the fundamental values of Christian life?

Translated by Mortimer Bear

Notes

1. For the relationship between Christianity and democracy cf. J. Maritain, *Christianity and Democracy* (1942), London 1944; J. Morienval, 'Democratie Chrétienne', *Catholicisme* 3, 1952, 585–93; L. Bedeschi, 'Democrazia cristiana', *Dizionario storico del movimento cattolico in Italia 1860–1980*, Turin 1981, 1/2, 246–57. It is interesting that so recent a manual as A. Anton, *El misterio de la Iglesia*, Madrid 1986–7, discusses the 'democratization of the church' only in terms of the Middle Ages, in connection with Marsilio and Ockham (although B. Tierney has shown the monarchical inspiration of the latter!). For the Protestant point of view cf. *Kirche und moderne Demokratie*, ed. T. Strohm and H.-D. Wendland, Darmstadt 1973.

2. Cf. J. Gaudemet, *Les élections dans l'Eglise latine des origines au XVIᵉ siècle*, Paris 1979, which distinguishes between 'choice' which has symbolic significance, and 'election', which in the modern sense implies not only the determination of the person but also the conferring of power.

3. Cf. the classic article by Y. Congar, *'Quod omnes tangit, ab omnibus tractari et approbari debet'*, *Revue historique de droit français et étranger* 36, 1958, 210–69.

4. For the council of Constance and its decree *Haec sancta* cf. my *Chiesa conciliare. Identità e significato del conciliarismo*, Brescia 1981, above all 187–240.

5. Cf. *Foi populaire et foi savante*, Paris 1976, and J. Sancho Bielsa, *Infallibilidad del pueblo de dios*, Pamplona 1979.

6. There was a debate during the 1970s, albeit mainly at an ideological level: K. Rahner, 'Demokratie in der Kirche?', *Stimmen der Zeit* 182, 1968, 1ff.; J. Ratzinger and H. Maier, *Demokratie in der Kirche. Möglichkeiten, Grenzen, Gefahren*, Limburg 1970; *Democratization of the Church*, *Concilium* 1971/3, and above all K. Lehmann, 'On the Dogmatic Justification for a Process of Democratization in the Church', ibid., 60–86; G. May, *Demokratisierung der Kirche. Möglichkeiten und Grenzen*, Vienna and Munich 1971; *Democratizzazione della chiesa. Memorandum del circolo cattolico di Bensberg*, Bologna 1972; M. Krämer, *Kirche kontra Demokratie? Gesellschaftliche Probleme in gegenwärtigen Katholizismus*, Munich 1973. There is a synthetic and updated presentation in K.-F. Daiber, 'Democratie. II.Praktisch-theologisch', *TRE* 8, 1981, 452–9.

7. Cf. my 'Dal bastone alla misericordia. Il magistero nel cattolicesimo contemporaneo (1830–1980)', in *La chiesa nella storia*, Brescia 1988, 240–73.

8. Cf. H. J. Pottmeyer, 'Lo sviluppo della teologia dell'ufficio papale nel contesto ecclesiologico, sociale e ecumenico nel XX secolo', in *Chiesa e Papato nel mondo contemporaneo*, ed. G. Alberigo and A. Riccardi, Rome and Bari 1990, 3–63; G. Alberigo, 'Le concezioni della Chiesa e i mutamenti istituzionali', ibid., 65–121.

9. The monarchical nature of the church and its character as an unequal society, 'that is, made up of two categories of persons, the pastors and the flock', were the supporting pillars of the official ecclesiology; see the encyclical *'Vehementer nos'* of 11 February 1906, *Acta Pii X*, 3, 34.

10. The best summary is that of J. M. R. Tillard, *Eglise d'Eglises*, Paris 1987.

11. Cf. Y. Congar, 'Status Ecclesiae', *Studia Gratiana* 15, 1972, 1–31.

12. Cf. Y. Congar, '*Ius divinum*', *Revue de droit canonique* 18, 1978, 108–22, and P. F. Fransen, 'Criticism of some Basic Theological Notions in Matters of Church Authority', in *Authority in the Church*. ed. P. F. Fransen, Louvain 1983, 48–74, which above all criticizes the ideological use of *jus divinum*.

13. After the conciliar debate at Vatican II on the members of the church and the universal priesthood, theological reflection has failed adequately to deepen and develop the pointers given by the council.

14. Nor has satisfactory progress been made after Vatican II on the theology of the people of God; cf. *Concilium* 176, *The People of God and the Poor* (in the English-language edition this issue oddly has on the cover *La Iglesia Popular: Between Fear and Hope*).

15. For what was originally a close connection between election and consecration cf. L. Mortari, *Consacrazione episcopale e collegialità*, Florence 1969.

16. There are the makings of a pointer in this direction in the Liturgical Constitution of Vatican II, *Sacrosanctum Concilium*.

17. Cf. A. Vauchez, *La sainteté en Occident aux derniers siècles du Moyen Age*, Rome 1981, and recently K. L. Woodward, *Making Saints: How the Catholic Church Determines Who Becomes a Saint, Who Doesn't, and Why*, New York 1990.

18. In connection with Newman cf. J. Walgrave, 'Newman's "On Consulting the Faithful in Matters of Doctrine"', *Concilium* 180, 1985, 23–30, and also R. Bergeron, *Les abus de l'église d'après Newman*, Tournai and Montreal 1971. Cf. also J. M. R. Tillard, 'A propos du *sensus fidelium*', *Proche Orient Chrétien* 25, 1975, 113–34; T. E. Gregory, Vox populi. *Popular Opinion and Violence in the Religious Controversies of the Fifth Century AD*, Columbus 1979; and P. Granfield, 'The *sensus fidelium* in the Episcopal Selection', *Concilium* 137, 1980, 33–38.

19. Cf. J. A. Coriden, 'The Canonical Doctrine of *receptio*', *The Jurist* 50, 1990, 58–82, and, more generally, *Election – Consensus – Reception, Concilium* 8/1972.

20. Cf. W. Beinert, 'Bedeutung und Begründung des Glaubensinnes (*sensus fidei*) als eines dogmatischen Erkenntniskriteriums', *Catholica* 25, 1971, 271–303; L. Sartori, 'What is the Criterion for the *Sensus Fidelium?*', *Concilium* 149, 1981; L. Swidler, 'Demokratia. The Rule of the People of God or *Consensus fidelium*', in *Authority in the Church* (n. 12), 226–43, and *The Teaching Authority of Believers*, *Concilium* 180, 1985.

21. Cf. J. Neumann, *Synodales Prinzip. Der Grössere Spielraum im Kirchenrecht*, Freiburg 1973.

22. Cf. L. Vischer, 'Drawn and Held Together by the Reconciling Power of Christ', *Ecumenical Review* 26, 1974, 166–90; R. Mehl, 'L'unité conciliaire de l'Église', in *Die Einheit der Kirche. Dimensionen ihrer Heiligkeit, Katholizität und Apostolozität. Festgabe P. Meinhold*, ed. L. Hein, Wiesbaden 1977, 69–79; H. M. Biedermann, 'Die Synodalität. Prinzip der Verfassung und Leitung der Orthodoxen Kirchen und Kirche', ibid., 296–314; W. Beinert, 'Konziliarität der Kirche. Ein Beitrag zur ökumenischen Epistemologie', *Catholica* 33, 1979, 81–108.

23. From the institutional point of view, the most interesting pole after the conclusion of the Council seems to be the development of the conferences of bishops. Not only have these significantly increased in number, but above all they have acquired an effective prestige, on many occasions being points of reference both for the life of the local churches and for relations with non-Catholic Christians and with society. A further indication of the importance of this institution is the lively discussion now current about its nature, its powers and its procedures, cf. *Naturaleza y futuro de las conferencias episcopales*, ed. H. Legrand, J. Manzaneres and A. Garcia y Garcia, Salamanca 1988, and *Die Bishopfskonferenzen. Theologischer und juridischer Status*, ed. H. Müller and H. J. Pottmeyer, Düsseldorf 1989.

24. The post-conciliar institutional reforms have also affected the local churches,

above all through the creation of collegial and representative organs such as presbyteral and pastoral councils. Very often these organs have a limited effect and not much of an impact, not enough at any rate to bring about the ecclesiological renewal expressed by Vatican II. One large-scale phenomenon has been the spread in Latin America of the 'basic communities', which seem to be the one extant form of parish renewal, cf. L. Boff, *Ecclesiogenesis*, Maryknoll and London 1986.

25. In the decisions of Vatican II, *participatio* recurs constantly in the Constitution *Sacrosanctum Concilium* on the liturgy and in the Constitution *Gaudium et spes* at nos. 431, *'De responsibilitate et participatione'* and 75, *'De omnium in vita publica cooperatione'*. Cf. P. Delooz, 'Comment évaluer les tentatives de participation dans l'église catholique?', *Pro mundi vita* 1984 (January 1981), 1–37, and G. Schwan, 'Partizipation', in *Christlicher Glaube in moderner Gesellschaft* 11, Freiburg 1981, 41–78.

26. Cf. Y. Congar, *I Believe in the Holy Spirit*, London 1983, and also *Credo in Spiritum Sanctum* II, Rome 1983, above all the articles by De La Potterie, Schnackenburg, Faricy, Tillard, Moltmann and Citrini.

27. Clearly in contemporary societies with a democratic regime, and also in the church, participation is increasingly threatened by the enormous development of bureaucracy and the correlative bureaucratization of all aspects of social life.

28. Cf. J. A. Komonchak, 'El principio de subsidariedad y su pertinencia eclesiologica', in *Naturaleza y futuro de las conferencias episcopales*, 367–424.

A Consecrated Hierarchy –
An Obstacle to a Democratizating
of the Catholic Church

Willy Obrist

It is well known among theologians that in its structure the present-day constitution of the Catholic church is analogous to the state constitutions of the *ancien regime*. Moreover the tug-of-war between episcopalianism and papalism or between synodicalism and Roman centralism which runs like a scarlet thread through church history has its analogy in the state sphere: in the tendency towards regional princely rule or an aristocratic republic on the one hand and the tendency towards absolute monarchy on the other.

The consecrated nobility

Now regardless of which tendency gained the upper hand, authority – legislative, executive and judicial – always lay in the hands of the nobility. If in the ancient states this was a nobility based on blood or service, in the Catholic church it was (and is) a consecrated nobility. Thus bishops and popes together form the higher nobility which here, as once in the state sphere, has the say and occupies the key positions.

The preservation or reproduction of the nobility varies between the state and the church and is yet analogous. Whereas aristocracy by blood reproduced itself through physical descendants, the consecrated nobility reproduces itself in a spiritual succession by the bestowing and receiving of consecration. Here it is decisive that the higher nobility controls the bestowing of consecration and that the full *potestas sacra* is handed on only in the consecration of bishops. In this way the spiritual higher nobility keeps a firm control of power. By handing down the 'sacred power' in the form of the ordination of priests and deacons the bishops then create or reproduce a lesser spiritual nobility; but by handing down the 'sacred power' only in a markedly diminished form, care is taken to keep this under control. On the other hand, the spiritual lesser nobility forms the reservoir from which candidates can be selected for consecration as bishops – to make good the number of the higher nobility. Moreover, the fact that in the end the pope, who according to church law is responsible to no one, decides who will become a bishop, is evidence of the absolutist structure of the present-day church: the fact that in the tug-of-war within the aristocratic society of the church during modern times papalism has come out on top. The possession of power was legitimated in the states of the *ancien régime*, as in the church, by the theory of rule by the grace of God. In the church this was supplemented by the sub-theory of the apostolic succession (which is historically untenable): by a theory which implies that the higher nobility of the church has received its power directly from the hand of the incarnate Son of God.

The presupposition for democratization

Now the category of *potestas sacra* is quite different from that of the authority of the nobility in the ancient states, since as well as pastoral authority (legislative, executive and judiciary) it also includes the power of consecration. In this characteristic of the *potestas sacra* lies the reason why so far no democratization has taken place within the Catholic church. If we are to reflect on whether such democratization is at all possible and if so, in what circumstances, we need first of all to take into account the presuppositions for the democratization of states. A first presupposition was mental: the replacement of the theory of rule by the grace of God with that of the sovereignty of the people. At first glance this would seem to mean secularization for the church, and that of course would be unacceptable. However, in my view the theory of the sovereignty of the people could be accepted while at the same time preserving that of the grace of God. Since Vatican II has described the church as a whole as the people of God and moreover has introduced the concept of universal priesthood, we could even speak of a sovereignty of the people by the grace of God. However, it was not a change in the theory of sovereignty that was decisive for the achivement of the democratization of the states. What was decisive was the removal of power from the nobility at every level, or, from the perspective of the nobility, the renunciation of its privileges of power. Could the consecrated nobility now be dispensed with in the Catholic church? That is the decisive question.

One element of 'sacred power' – pastoral authority – could be exercised by laity without further ado. If it were bestowed on officials in a democratic way by the people, along with all the other consequences this would bring the advantage that now at last legislative, executive and judiciary functions could also be separated in the Catholic church, which would correspond to a basic feature of present-day sensibility about the law.

Now apart from the two authorities which are distinguished in the canonistic tradition (now euphemistically designated *munus*), Vatican II also mentioned the teaching 'office'. There would be no problems if this, too, were exercised by lay theologians. However, it is very improbable that in a church with a democratic constitution spiritual supervision by a teaching authority would still be tolerated.

The characteristic element of *sacra potestas*, the power of consecration, is quite different from that of the pastoral and teaching authority. This is the real obstacle in the way of democratization. Moreover, maintaining this concept or making it tabu is the reason why the 'visible' Catholic church nowadays stands out in our democratic landscape like a fossil from a time long past. Despite all talk of the universal priesthood, it perpetuates the church caste of the nobility with all its privileges of power.

On closer inspection it is no longer possible to provide any basis for the concept of 'the power of consecration'. In simple terms, the power of consecration is the capacity to perform rites effectively. Thus the rite of ordination to the priesthood (according to the Catholic conception) makes the candidate capable of effectively performing the sacramental rites, with the exception of ordination. The rite of consecration to bishop then makes those chosen for this office capable of effectively performing the rite of ordination to the diaconate and the priesthood and also of episcopal consecration.

Now underlying the conception of the effectiveness of ritual action is a pattern of thought which is rooted in the archaic world-view: in an understanding of the self and the world which all in all has been overtaken in the evolutionary change in Western consciousness.

The archaic understanding of self and world

The term 'archaic world-view' in the sense meant here is a recent one. It arose in the 1970s in the concern to work out a handy methodological approach to research into the evolution of consciousness. The new feature of this approach was the quest for a criterion by which the level of evolution of a culture could be defined. When such a criterion was found in the capacity specific to human beings to distinguish between I and not-I, and this was applied to material from the history of culture, the first great difficulty that arose was the fact that people of former times understood the world as it is in quite a different way from the way in which we understand it now, and that they constructed patterns of action which no longer make any sense to us. If there was a concern to find out what capacity for distinction was expressed in an earlier culture it was necessary first of all to grasp how the structure of the world was understood then, in all its inner logic.

To begin with, people faced a variety of different cultures. In view of the fact that the bio-evolution could only be reconstructed once comparative anatomy, physiology, embryology etc., had showed that a common pattern (spontaneity, assimilation of information, material change, reproduction, etc.) underlay the tremendous multiplicity of living beings, the question arose whether such a basic pattern could not also be worked out for the earlier cultures. From the interdisciplinary transcultural comparison it then emerged that in fact all previous cultures, including that of our own Middle Ages, had a basic characteristic pattern of understanding themselves and the world: a pattern which, while varying widely in geographical distribution and over the course of time, remained unchanged in its basic structure down to the beginning of modern times. This pattern was then termed archaic, to distinguish it from the categorically different patterns of today. Characteristic of the archaic view of the world is a dualism between this world and another world, between nature and supernature, immanence and transcendence. It was assumed that the other world was inhabited by invisible beings. Two categories of these were distinguished: autochthonous beings (gods and intermediate beings) and the 'dead who live on'. Three capacities were attributed to the other world: the capacity to have an effect on this world through mere will (without making use of the natural chains of cause and effect), the capacity to incarnate itself, and finally the capacity to communicate itself to human beings.

This kind of communication was called (supernatural) revelation. According to archaic ideas, revelation could come either from the beyond (by means of an 'appearance' or 'rapture' or by 'inspiration'), or through an incarnate spiritual being speaking 'man to man'. The idea that beings from the other world could have an influence on this world also led to the idea that the divine will was made known through natural events (omens) and through the fate that these decided for individuals or for whole peoples (revelation of history).

Archaic men and women attributed all knowledge about the other world and the will of the other world to such a process of revelation. For them it was the *physically* true substance of faith; today we speak of *psychologic-ally* true religious myths, understanding myths as forms of the uncon-scious, i.e. as linguistic representations of real psychological powers or circumstances. Knowledge of events in this world – to use a present-day expression – was also largely mythical. If early man asked questions which he did not have the cognitive means for answering, forms of the unconscious poured out (projected themselves) over his head into the vacuum in knowledge. Thus in archaic cultures there were historical myths or mythical historiography, and myths to explain nature or mythical theories about natural events; mythical cosmogonies and cosmologies, mythical doctrines of descent (one example is the Old Testament 'account' of creation), mythical anatomies, physiologies etc.

Archaic conceptions of space, time and causality also differed from ours. The conception of space was qualitative and dynamic. As the unconscious psychological process was still largely perceived in projection, particular places were regarded as points for the breaking in of the beyond, as places of theophany (a qualitative experience of space). For the same reason, people believed that the ingredients of this world could change unpredict-ably at any time (a dynamic experience of space). The conception of time was in terms of the present, as this corresponds to immediate experience, possibly even cyclical, corresponding to experience of the seasons and the (apparent) cyclical motion of the stars. Finally, the reason for a change in things was seen in what we would now call the acausal effect of powers having thoughts and wills: an effect which emanated either from human beings or from the other world.

The rite: a typically archaic pattern of behaviour

This conception of effective power led to two typical patterns of behaviour, magic and rite. Whereas magic can be described as a purely human accomplishment through demonstration and prompting, ritual action can be described as activity aided by metaphysical beings. However, in ceremonies both great and small, over wide stretches of the evolution of consciousness, we find rites and magic interwoven; here a predominance of magical elements is an expression of lower phylogenetic awareness.

The ritual pattern of action consisted in the abbreviated and symbolic description or dramatization in a prescribed way of saving actions of other-worldly beings of whom people thought that they had knowledge through revelation. Underlying this action was the idea (quite logical in the framework of an archaic view of the world) that the pronouncing of prescribed texts and the carrying out of prescribed actions caused what beings of the other world 'once' did there or during a visit to earth to happen 'now' (an expression of a presentistic conception of time).

Although the ritual pattern of behaviour in principle remained un-altered, the shaping and application of rites formed a process which is described as the evolution of consciousness during the archaic phase. In early stages there were only imperfect distinctions between inward and outward and between animate and inanimate. As the unconscious psychological process was still experienced almost exclusively in terms of external projection, for people of that time striking things and natural phenomena also had an 'other worldly' dimension, a 'side' which was also experienced as a person from the other world (natural spirit). From this stage of the evolution of the consciousness, which is often called magical or animistic, we are able – through a long and complex sequence of cultures, which also involve re-archaizings – to observe one great movement: the elevation of heaven. As heaven was increasingly removed from the things of 'this' world and shifted into the distance, the dualism of this world and the beyond was expressed increasingly clearly. In the process, clearly demarcated and predominantly religious myths came into being which told of the actions of the inhabitants of heaven. The metaphysical populations which were still very extensive in 'natural religions' were reduced, and hand in hand with this tendency to monotheism, religious myths became increasingly less fantastic and less gross.

The development of dualism was further supported by a qualitative change in the other world: whereas this had originally been imagined as having as it were the same consistency as this world (experienced in dynamistic terms), now it was increasingly imagined as being less material. This dematerializing of the other world and its inhabitants and of the human soul led to the idea of the spiritual, or the distinction between matter and spirit. Parallel to this process came an increasing capacity for distinguishing in what happened under heaven (= in this world). Here the predominantly qualitative conception of space was replaced by a three-dimensional sense, and things were increasingly experienced as permanent. The presentistic and cyclical experience of time was overlaid with a linear one, extending into past and future.

What persisted longest was the conception of the acausal achievement of changes through personal powers. This was only overcome in modern times by the development of the natural sciences. In the concern to penetrate behind the façade of mere appearance, science developed the concept of causality. The notion of causality certainly changed over the course of time: from the rigidly linear through the statistical (in the microsphere) to that of a retrocoupled network. But the concept of causality was always quite a different category from the notion of the influence of powers from the other world and the influence which underlies magical practices and rites. However, as thinking in terms of powers was overcome *outside* the church sphere, ritual action could survive unassailed within it right down to our time.

Nevertheless, in the course of the evolution of consciousness the notion of what ritual activity was for necessarily changed. If every year the creation myth 'had' to be dramatized at a lower level to bring about the ongoing existence of the world, since the world had 'a tendency to lapse into chaos', and if furthermore people 'had to' bring about salvation for their harvest, for their herds, their fishing, for battles, and so on (usually by performing the actions of an incarnate cultural hero), those rites gradually gained the upper hand by which the salvation of souls was to be achieved. The sacramental rites of the Catholic church were the ripest fruit of this development.

The idea of how the celebrant was involved in ritual activity also changed in the course of time. The belief that during the sacral action the celebrant was the metaphysical being whose acts he dramatized (something which can still be demonstrated, for example, among the Maya) was certainly the expression of a low phylogenetic consciousness. But the celebrant was always regarded as a being of a special kind in the sense of being ontologically other. It is hard for us to follow how people imagined this otherness – just as it is hard for us to grasp the whole archaic experience of the world. At all events it implied the conception of a capacity for acausal activity, a capacity which the 'ordinary person' did not possess. For this reason, according to Catholic doctrine only the priest can make Christ 'really present', e.g. by pronouncing words of transformation, and not the laity.

In many cultures this otherness persisted only for the time that someone celebrated a rite. At a primitive stage the celebrant was 'transformed' into a being who had power to bring this about by being painted, by donning a mask or putting on a headdress, and later by the wearing of insignia (which similarly had a basis in the myth). In the Catholic church this otherness is effected by a rite – the rite of consecration or ordination – and then 'persists' for the whole duration of the priest's life. The idea of what according to Catholic doctrine is effected by the rite of consecration or ordination found linguistic expression in the term *character indelebilis*. The distinction between clergy and laity in canon law, and as it is also laid down in the new Codex, has its foundation in this thoroughly archaic conception. It is the basis for the concept of *potestas sacra*, with all its effects on the constitution of the 'visible' church. At present there is certainly a tendency to blur the archaic character of the status of the clergy or the consecrated nobility by the use of the expression 'office' (priestly office, episcopal office). However, it should specifically be pointed out that the bestowing of *potestas sacra* is something fundament-ally different from the bestowing of an office in the secular sphere or in the Protestant and Reformed church.

Let us remember that the ordained priesthood remains the exception in inter-cultural comparisons. Since in most cultures the rites that convey salvation are carried out by individuals who are not consecrated, and since Vatican II has now declared the *universal* priesthood, it would now be conceivable to abolish the consecrated priesthood and thus the power and privileges of the consecrated nobility while retaining the archaic world-view. The Protestant churches (at least the Protestant Reformed churches) have already demonstrated that this would open up the way for a real democratization. The reason why the Protestant churches have democratic constitutions today is that the Reformation threw the ordained priesthood overboard. That liberated these churches from an early archaic pattern of behaviour, but they have nevertheless been able to remain within the archaic world-view down to the present day by retaining the archaic conception of revelation. This concept was certainly all right at that time. Although the Reformation can be seen in retrospect as a deposition of the archaic world-view, at that time the evolution of consciousness had not yet progressed to the stage that the archaic world-view could have been replaced by an equivalent world-view at a higher level of evolution. Today, however, the situation is different. In the course of modernity an evolutionary change in our understanding of ourselves and the world has taken place – outside the church and theology – in which the dualistic world-view which had been valid since the Stone Age has been replaced by a differentiated *unistic* (not monistic!) world-view. This no longer differentiates between a material 'this world' and an immaterial 'other world' inhabited by spiritual beings but – thanks to the achievements of complementary thinking – between a material and a spiritual aspect of the reality of space and time, which is one in itself.

Research into the evolution of consciousness

It became possible to recognize clearly with what amazing consistency this change took place, what had *essentially* changed, and how as a result a real evolutionary step had been taken from a naive to a differ-entiated world-view when during the 1970s a handy methodological approach to research into the evolution of consciousness had finally been discovered.

For a long time there had already been talk of the evolution of consciousness, usually under the concept of 'cultural evolution'. However, previous schemes could not withstand the criticism of those for whom the evolution of consciousness was a thorn in the flesh. Nor were they able to grasp the heart of the matter by their methodological approach. The reason for this was that the attention of researchers was exclusively directed to cultural phenomena, and not to the cognitive system that produces culture, to consciousness. However, this had to be considered first if it were to prove possible to get at the heart of the problem.

Now evolution, i.e. the increase in the complexity of a system, can only be demonstrated if one knows the basic properties of that system. So it was necessary first of all to discover what we understand by consciousness in the present state of knowledge. Philosophical epistemology and scientific psychology alone were incapable of discovering this. What did prove competent, however, was research into evolutionary biological cognition: that trend of research within the new biology which investigates the progressive increase in complexity in unconscious cognitive systems, from single cells to the primates.

Here an insight gained in the transition from the mechanistic to the systemic consideration of nature was of decisive significance: the insight that in the step from a simpler to a more complex system – in the integration of partial systems which had previously functioned independently into a 'higher system' with a unified function – completely new properties come into existence. The question of the characteristic properties of consciousness was thus tantamount to the question what cognitive capacities came into existence or were added to previous already highly complex cognitive capacities when the step was taken from animal primates to human beings, i.e. from unconscious to unconscious-conscious living beings. The result was, as I have indicated, the capacity to distinguish between I and not-I. That meant on the one hand that human beings could detach themselves from involvement or physical participation in the species-specific environment characteristic of unconscious living beings and could realize that they themselves were separate from this environment, and on the other that it became possible for them to make distinctions in the not-I (objective reality), to recognize regularities, and as a result to penetrate behind the façade of mere appearances.

It was possible to recognize whether this capacity increased progressively, i.e. whether a real evolution of the consciousness had taken place, by investigating the cultures known to us to see what degree of capacity to distinguish between I and not-I is expressed in them.

The mutation of consciousness

It proved that this capacity already increased progressively against the background of the archaic world-view, less on the physical than on the metaphysical branch; less by grappling with 'this world' than by 'grappling' with the other world, i.e. through theological reflection.

But it also emerged that towards the end of our Middle Ages this development reached its ceiling; after that a major step in evolution took place in the sense of a systemic leap, in which a completely new way was found of understanding those experiencable powers which archaic human beings understood as beings from another world. It proved that there were *already powers* (dynamisms) of the unconscious sphere of the psyche, inaccessible to the consciousness, which were seen in visions (in 'appearances' and 'raptures') and great dreams or in aniconic evidence (the idea of a being who created the world, i.e. the God of the philosophers, was not affected by this). Since research into the reciprocal relationship between consciousness and unconsciousness we can also see why these forms of the unconscious were also understood (perceived) in concrete terms: not as metaphorical manifestations of psychological powers but as concrete persons from the 'other world' (cf. W. Obrist, *Concilium*, 1983).

However, research into the evolution of consciousness also showed that in this evolutionary step not only was the archaic world-view superseded but also the positivistic, atheistic and areligious world-view of 'modernity'; that this was only a (necessary) transitional stage and that – through the discovery of the species-specific unconscious (what Jung called the 'collective' unconscious) – it was then superseded, along with the archaic stage, so that at this second stage the religious dimension has again been fully disclosed, albeit with a new understanding of religion.

This is not the place to describe the consequences this mutation of consciousness will have for theology and the church. At any rate, the change of world-view will only be assimilated into the general consciousness in stages. However, it is certain that first of all this process of assimilation will see the elimination of that already largely emptied, early archaic thought-pattern from which ritual action or sacramentalism first emerged, and with it the idea of the 'power of consecration'. The obstacle which so far has blocked a democratization of the Catholic church will then disappear.

Many people will feel the surrender of ritual action as a loss. However, the great gain which would be brought by the democratization of the church must be set over against this. This would, for example, make it possible for the individual particular churches again to develop as before in accordance with their social and cultural environment; it would also bring with it the possibility of a revival of spirituality which has largely died out, at least in the Western church, under the pressure of hypertrophied and fossilized structures and the rigid maintaining of an obsolete world-view. However, this would be a spirituality which was at the level of consciousness of present-day men and women.

Translated by John Bowden

II · Examples

(a)   From Tradition

Reception, Consensus and Church Law

Geoffrey King

Reception and consensus are two aspects of the one reality. Both speak of decision-making as a corporate activity, involving a body of people (in the case of reception, potentially the whole body of the church). Consensus is usually thought of as coming before the promulgation of a decision, reception as coming after. The reality is more complex. Consensus and reception intertwine: one need think only of the commonsense view that people are more likely to receive a decision if they have been involved in shaping it. In fact, effective decision occurs when the consensus that has shaped it meets with the consensus of the receiving community.

Even so, here I shall treat consensus and reception separately, beginning with reception and concentrating on reception of church law.

Reception

The doctrine of reception of law finds its first clear formulation in the *Decretum* of Gratian. Much of the subsequent reflection on reception is found in commentary on his *dictum* (D.4, c.3):

Laws are instituted when promulgated; they are confirmed (strengthened) when approved by the *mores* of those who use them (put them into practice).

A clue to Gratian's meaning is given by the context. He has just cited the description of law attributed to Isidore of Seville:

> A law will be honest, just, possible, in accord with nature, in accord with the customs of the country, suitable to place and time, necessary, useful, clear so that it does not through obscurity contain something unsuitable, not for any private benefit, but for the common usefulness of the citizens.

The implication, then, is that non-reception is a sign that one or more of these qualities is lacking. That is, Gratian was concerned with the intrinsic qualities of a law rather than its extrinsic authority (the authority that comes from the official position of the lawgiver). This is confirmed by the broader context – Gratian is discussing the finality and quality of laws, not conflicts between legal authorities. And Gratian's whole attitude to the authority of the Roman See makes it inconceivable that he would set up popular sovereignty in competition with it.[1]

Failure to appreciate Gratian's concentration on intrinsic authority would bedevil later discussion of reception. If one thinks of non-reception as an act of one external authority ('the people') in opposition to another external authority (the ecclesiastical lawgiver), little progress is possible. But if non-reception is taken as a possible sign of the intrinsic inadequacy of the law, a very different result can emerge. The earliest (Decretist) commentators on Gratian discuss approval by the practices of the users mainly in the context of consultation prior to the law's general promulgation, that is, in the context of the extrinsic authority of law.[2] But they also consider the intrinsic authority of laws. Huguccio and the *Summa Reginensis* take the case of a dispute arising in consistory between pope and cardinals. For both writers, the will of the pope should usually prevail: he has the greater (extrinsic) authority. But intrinsic authority also has its place. The pope's will should not prevail if it is contrary to the law and the gospel (*Summa Reginensis*) or contrary to reason or to the Old or New Testament (Huguccio).

Johannes Teutonicus makes a parallel concession in the case of a bishop who had unsuccessfully argued against a proposed law. He should submit to the pope's judgment, unless the pope is acting *contra fidem* (*fides* in the sense not of dogmatic definitions but of the general good of the church).

Huguccio takes the further step of considering rejection of a law after it has been approved by pope and cardinals. The pope has plenitude of power: can he not compel obedience? He can do so, replies Huguccio, when clergy and people are acting contrary to faith or reason. Otherwise, he should not. Huguccio appears to allow for reasonable refusal to accept a papal law, a refusal which is effective and which does not diminish the pope's plenitude of power. Is it the case that papal coercion is inappropriate because of some defect intrinsic to the law? If so, that would imply the right of clergy and people to judge even papal laws on their intrinsic merits.

Only one commentator (Matthaeus Romanus) seems to have gone so far as to make reception an essential element in the establishment of a law. The three requisites for such establishment he lists as institution, promulgation and approval by the practices of its users.

An early Decretist gloss (the *Glossa Palatina*) offered a distinction. Reception is required for the *de facto* confirmation of a law; *de iure* a law is confirmed in its very institution. The significance of such a distinction depends on the weight that one gives to the two kinds of confirmation. *De iure* confirmation can be seen as all-important and the *de facto* as only a desirable embellishment. A more realistic approach will see *de iure* confirmation as meaning merely that the law is 'on the books'. *De facto* confirmation is needed to transform this lifeless letter into a vital force within the community.

An interpretation close to that which I have attributed to Gratian comes from the fifteenth-century canonist/ecclesiologist Juan de Torquemada. Torquemada was a staunch anti-conciliarist, but he allowed for the possibility of the vote of bishops in council outweighing a proposed papal law. He offers an example: if the pope tried to depose all the bishops in the world, his decree would be harmful and should not be accepted. In this case the subjects have the power to contradict the superior, not because of their greater (extrinsic) authority but because of the bad quality of the law (*non ex maioritate auctoritatis, sed ex ipsa mala qualitate legis*).

A similar style of argumentation can be seen in interpretations which take their cue from the Isidorian 'in accord with the customs of the country' (*secundum consuetudinem patriae*). Jean Gerson, in a passage in no way dependent on his 'concilliar' views, argued for the need to adapt laws to the time, place and circumstances of their subjects, 'because a law which is useful for one time and place, might be impossible or harmful in another time or place or for other people'. He sees reception as a sign of such usefulness. Even in the late eighteenth century Joseph Ponsius argued that some laws were never received in certain territories because they were ill-adapted to circumstances of time and place or to the *indoles* of a particular nation. In the early seventeenth century Martin Becanus, starting from more explicitly voluntarist principles, had reached similar conclusions. He argued that the pope, when legislating, wishes to take account of local circumstances and to respect local customs. If a law fails to do so – and this becomes apparent when the law is not accepted by a particular community – one presumes that the pope does not know local circumstances, and that he would change the law if he did know them. Thus the law does not oblige. At least in the arguments of Ponsius and Bacanus, non-reception by the particular community does not constitute the law's lack of suitability for that community: rather, it is a sign of the absence of suitability.

Other commentators (Joannes Driedo, Gregory of Valencia) argue that laws which a community finds unacceptable will be the source of disturbance rather than of the common good, will be dangerous rather than useful, destructive rather than constructive (*in aedificationem*). Such arguments seem to recognize that for laws to be effective they must somehow commend themselves to the community. A law may be based on sound theological and legal principles, may have a good purpose, may be clearly formulated. But if it cannot commend itself, it remains at best a good idea, not a good law. For the whole purpose of a law is to lead to action. It is possible, for example, to be opposed to the consumption of alcohol but to consider that the Prohibition laws in the United States were bad laws. Again, it is a matter of non-reception being a sign of a deficiency in the law (or at least in the way in which the law is communicated to people).

Other interpretations of Gratian are of less concern to us here. For instance, it was commonly argued that a non-received law is more quickly shaken by contrary custom than is a law once received and later disobeyed. Or again, it was argued that, when the majority of a community is disobeying a law, it is unfair to impose it on the 'virtuous' few. Hence, there is no moral obligation for the few to follow the law. But the issue here is obscured by a confusion of law and morality, a legalistic approach to morality.

Even so brief a summary indicates that reception was frequently seen as a necessary part of effective law-making from the time of Gratian to at least the late eighteenth century. Those who espoused such theories were for the most part people of unquestioned orthodoxy, and in the mainstream of a generally conservative canonical tradition. From the late eighteenth century until comparatively recently, however, reception almost disappeared from canonical discussion. Twentieth-century canonists either fail to mention it, treat it as a museum piece, or, like Cicognani, denounce it as a theory of 'regalists, Protestants and Gallicans' based on a 'false and equivocal' interpretation of Gratian.

Cicognani, in fact, gives us the clue to one of the reasons why reception fell into disfavour. It became associated with Gallicanism and Febronianism, and hence entangled in the church-state conflicts of eighteenth- and nineteenth-century Europe.

The second reason, I suggest, was the prevalence of voluntarist attitudes to law. I will examine each of these factors in turn.

Gallican and Febronian writers adopted a strong version of reception theory. Pierre de Marca, for instance, in his *de Libertatibus Ecclesiae Gallicanae*, stated simply that the prince has the power to make laws, but that they are not binding until they have been accepted by the judgment of the people. The Four Articles of the French clergy (1682) had concluded with the general proposition that the pope's judgment 'is not irreformable unless the consent of the church has been given'. Reaction to this proposition was to play a crucial part in the formulation of the infallibility definition of Vatican I. But reactions were also directed against the notion of reception of law.

The church-state entanglement is particularly evident in the theories of Johann Nikolaus von Hontheim ('Febronius'), who depicted the pope as proposing laws and the church as deciding whether to accept the proposals. He argued for the legitimacy of the royal *placet* with regard to church laws. The views of Febronius found practical expression in the policies of the Austrian emperor Joseph II. In 1781 Joseph declared all papal decrees, whether disciplinary or doctrinal, subject to the imperial *placet*. This declaration was merely one item in an overall plan for the reform of the church, a plan drawn up on the supposition that the church was subordinate to the state.

None of this affects the substance of Gratian's *dictum* or the validity of the views of those who commented on it. Moreover, the situation of pre-revolutionary or Napoleonic France or of the Austrian empire at the end of the eighteenth century has no parallels in most parts of the church today. But guilt by association is a powerful force, and reception theory suffered from such guilt for a long time. Indeed, when the Inquisition under Alexander VII issued (in 1665) an apparent condemnation of a version of reception theory, the condemnation was really directed against Gallican claims rather than against reception as such.[3]

The other part of the context inimical to reception theory was the prevailing voluntarist attitude to law. Voluntarism sees the authority of a law as coming from the authority of the lawgiver. It is an extrinsic view of legal authority (as distinct from the view which sees the authority of law as coming from its intrinsic authority, its possessing the qualities listed, for instance, in the Isidorian description). For a voluntarist, to give any decisive weight to reception is to pit one 'extrinsic' authority ('the people') against another extrinsic authority (the ecclesiastical lawgiver, which for the universal church usually means the pope). When the question is posed in that way, non-reception is likely to be seen simply as disobedience. On the other hand, greater attention to the intrinsic authority of law enables us to avoid seeing reception as part of an unproductive conflict between rulers and ruled. It becomes possible to acknowledge that the church community may perceive that a given law is not useful or reasonable or not attuned to the conditions of a particular country. Non-reception may be an expression of that perception.

Viewed from this point of view, reception can be seen to command even more support in the canonical tradition than is apparent from the list of interpretations already given. Almost all canonists admit that a law is not a true law unless it meets the requirements listed in the Isidorian description. The Decretist Richardus Anglicus provides an early example. A law can 'fail' because its purpose has ceased, because of regional variations, because it is excessively rigorous, because it provides an occasion for evil-doing or is otherwise counterproductive. Others will add that a law which is unjust, unreasonable, *inutilis*, or morally impossible to observe is no law. Of course, some of these canonists leave it to the lawgiver to decide whether a law is thus defective. But others put more trust in the community. Even Suarez, the 'Prince of Voluntarists', allows that we can see that a law's purpose has ceased when this is the consensus of the community. The nineteenth-century moralist Gury puts it more positively. The *sanior pars* of a community would not reject a law without good reason. He goes on:

> The reason is clear, because the *sanior pars* of the people is made up of learned, trustworthy and prudent people. These people and the many who follow them would not find a law repugnant unless they had reason to fear that grave difficulties or scandal or disturbance would result from it.

If then we can escape from the distraction of Gallicanism and from the narrowness of vision induced by voluntarism, we may be able to see that law-making is a process – a process involving communication of values and strategies (ends and means) and issuing in common action. Genuine communication involves dialogue, not monologue. Reception may then be seen as a response to the initiative taken by the lawgiver in promulgation. It may confirm, call for modification of, or sometimes call entirely into question, the values or strategies chosen. The difficulty, of course, is that this is often an inarticulate response, which is too easily mistaken by the lawgiver for unreflective compliance or unreflective disobedience. But inarticulate-ness is not necessarily the product of lack of reflection. It may easily result from lack of channels of communication. A response, no matter how inarticulate, and whether positive or negative, needs to be seen precisely as a response, one step in the process of dialogue.

Further work is needed to understand the response, to discover what it is saying about the community and about the law that has been promulgated. Reception is a complex process of formation, discernment, and dialogue.

The idea of reception, then, offers little support to democracy in the church, if democracy is taken in a narrow sense of the power of the people (in potential conflict with the power of the rulers). But if democracy means a church where the whole church community contributes to the shaping of the church's life, then reception is an important aspect of that contribution.

Consensus

All that has been said so far concerns the response of a community after a law has been promulgated. Common sense suggests, however, that the response (common action) is more likely to be positive if the community has been involved in the formulation of the law (the articulation of values and discovery of strategies) before promulgation.

In fact, many of the earliest commentators on Gratian's *Decretum* discuss 'approval by the practices of the users' in terms of discussion before the promulgation. Johannes Teutonicus sees this discussion taking place among the bishops. Sicard of Cremona, the *Summa Reginensis* and Huguccio see it taking place among the cardinals. The *Glossa Palatina* puts it more strongly: the pope cannot make a general law *de statu universali ecclesiae* without the cardinals.[4]

These views reflect a comparatively new situation in the church, namely the role in church governance of the college of cardinals. But this role can be seen as a restricted continuation of the synodal tradition of the first millennium. And in the coming centuries the role of the cardinals would continue to be discussed, especially in the context of 'corporation theory'.

The importance of synods and councils in the first millennium is obvious. It was in such assemblies that church discipline was regulated, major (and some minor) controversies resolved, doctrinal formulations arrived at. Much of the material in Gratian's *Decretum* comes from synods and councils, including series of councils like those of Carthage and Toledo.

The close connection between council and consensus is, however, worth emphasis.[5] One of the earliest 'theorists' of the conciliar idea is Cyprian of Carthage. For Cyprian a key phrase in describing a council is 'to come together' (*in unum convenire*). This means more than a physical coming together of bishops; it is a coming together of minds and hearts, a reaching of consensus (*una consensio, commune consilium*). As Sieben has pointed out, Cyprian speaks also of a 'vertical' consensus to complement this 'horizontal' consensus. It involves agreement with the word of the Scriptures and with the tradition of the church concerned. 'The task of the council is now, on the basis of the consensus understood to have already been given, to achieve its own consensus.'[6] It was, moreover, not only a matter of achieving consensus during the meeting. Synods sent synodal letters to other churches, as a means of communicating information, but especially in order to invite others to associate themselves with the consensus reached.

The practice of sending synodal letters brings together the ideas of consensus and reception. The importance of a synod did not simply depend on the number and dignity of the bishops present, but on the extent to which its decrees were received. Indeed, reception is a crucial factor in determining which councils are to be considered ecumenical. It is difficult to find any criterion other than reception by which all the councils recognized as ecumenical by the Roman Catholic Church (from Nicaea to Vatican II) can be considered ecumenical. In this sense, reception can not only point to intrinsic authority but can constitute an extrinsic authority.

Over the centuries, the 'claims' of particular councils stand in some tension with the primatial claims of Rome. The attitude of Leo the Great, one of the first millennium's stronger proponents of primacy, is instructive. Leo frequently stresses the usefulness of synods, seeing them for instance as places where 'whatever controversial cases arise may be brought to an end by the help of the Lord so that no tension remains, but only the love which unites brothers more closely to one another'. He does not see himself as controlling councils of other churches but intervening only if other synods have failed to resolve a case. For his own church in Rome, Leo encouraged two synods each year. He writes of discussing questions objectively with the advice of all participants, so that truth could be found more securely. 'Thus did what came to us by a divine inspiration receive assent among the many assembled brothers.' This last remark suggests that it was more a matter of obtaining assent to Leo's proposals than of initiating open discussion, and certainly he saw the synod as a means of papal governance. But the 'balance of power' between pope and synod participants may well have been different in the case of popes less strong-willed or less competent than Leo.

The use of synods as a means of papal governance finds a new expression with another Leo (Leo IX) in a very different age (the mid-eleventh century). This first of the reforming popes travelled widely through Europe and used synods as a means of enforcing his reforming policies, demanding, for instance, confession on the part of simoniacal bishops.

These methods were carried further by the popes of the twelfth and thirteenth centuries who used general councils as means of asserting papal monarchy. At the same time, such popes saw it as important that councils represent the church. Boniface VIII cited the maxim *quod omnes tangit ab omnibus tractari et approbari debet* as demanding the presence at councils of the different estates of the Christian body. Here he stood firmly in the canonical tradition. Huguccio, the *Glossa Palatina* and the Ordinary Gloss all adduce *quod omnes tangit* as proving that, in decisions on matters of faith, even lay people should be represented. They were commenting on Gratian (D. 96 c. 4), where he stated that, since maintenance of the faith was a matter of universal concern, it pertained not only to clerics, but also to laity and indeed to every Christian. Earlier Innocent III summoned the Fourth Lateran Council, 'the greatest representative assembly of the mediaeval world'. It brought together 400 bishops, 800 abbots, representatives of cathedral chapters and other collegiate churches, envoys of the emperor-elect, of the kings of England, France and Hungary, and of some Italian cities. It was representative in the sense of being a microcosm of Christendom rather in the sense that its members were elected delegates (although this was the position of the representatives of collegiate bodies and of the Italian cities, while abbots were elected to their abbacies by their communities, and bishops were still the products of some electoral process in their dioceses).[7]

Centralization could, however, produce paradoxical results. It could provoke local protests, and assemblies originally summoned to enhance the authority of a ruler could become a place for giving corporate expression to such protests. Such a development is evident in the church at the fifteenth-century councils of Constance and Basel, but part of the ground for the development had been laid by canonical theories on corporations elaborated two centuries earlier.[8]

Since the mid-thirteenth century canonists had agreed that authority in a corporation resided in all the members, not just in the head. They debated at length the relations between head and members, but few disputed the fact that the head could not act without the consent of the members in important matters affecting the well-being of the whole corporation.[9] Hostiensis, perhaps the leading corporation theorist, consistently treated the Roman See, like any other bishopric, as subject to the normal rules of corporation law.[10] And at the heart of such treatment was the assumption of the underlying authority of the whole church, the *congregatio fidelium*.

Even the term *plenitudo potestatis* was interpreted in this light. It could, of course, be used as a support for absolute monarchy (and was so used by Innocent III and Innocent IV). But for many canonists (such as Huguccio) it had more the sense conveyed by the English 'plenipotentiary powers', that is, powers that are general, to a significant extent discretionary, but ultimately delegated. Huguccio had treated the *plena potestas* of the pope and that of a bishop as parallel, the difference being that that of the pope had a broader geographical extent, and such views were not forgotten even in the fourteenth century.[11]

The ideal of consensus remained of crucial importance at Vatican II. The conciliar constitutions and decrees were passed by majorities typically in the range of two thousand 'for' to one hundred 'against'. This was the result of procedures designed to obtain consensus. There was agreement that conciliar decisions call for a kind of moral unanimity. Hence there emerged procedural rules like that requiring a two-thirds majority of those present. This is a high standard, since it means that invalid votes or abstentions count effectively as negative votes. The result has been aptly termed a 'working consensus', a middle ground between a cosmetic consensus (a papering-over of major differences) and a complete synthesis.[12] Of course, this meant that different theologies appear side by side in the texts, while at times the council opted consciously for open-ended terms like *obsequium* (LG 25) and *subsistit* (LG 8).

The weaknesses of such a working consensus have become sometimes painfully apparent in recent years. Statements inserted in documents as a concession to an older theology can be taken from their context and offered as *the* conciliar teaching. We are witnessing attempts to close what was meant to be open-ended and to interpret it in a restrictive way. *Obsequium* is interpreted as total submission, and even *subsistit* is taken to mean the complete coincidence of the Church of Christ and the Roman Catholic Church. But these very real difficulties should not blind us to the achievement made possible by the working consensus. The council changed the church in profound ways. One wonders whether its decrees would have been so positively received if, for instance, they were passed by only very small majorities. Consensus facilitates reception.

The different models of consensus that I have sketched so briefly are clearly some distance removed from contemporary democratic models. They involve not simply majority vote, but the intersection of horizontal and vertical consensus. Those 'voting' in synods and councils are for the most part bishops: although for many centuries they were elected as bishops, they did not attend synods as elected representatives in the sense that modern members of parliaments are representatives of their constituents. Conciliar bodies can be manipulated by a strong 'executive' (a phenomenon not unknown in contemporary democracies). But the models of consensus are also far removed from any model of absolute monarchy. They embody the principle that major decisions in the life of the church should come from the church, and hence be precisely the product of consensus.

Thus far I have been discussing consensus in terms of what goes on before a decision is made. But for such a decision to be effective, indeed to be a decision rather than an intention, it must be received. The consensus reached in synod or council must meet with the consensus of the whole people of God, not in the sense of receiving juridical ratification, but in that of its being perceived as life-giving, of its being appropriated and so becoming part of the life of the church.

Notes

1. The ground-breaking research on this point was done by L. De Luca, 'L'accettazione popolare delle lege canonica nel pensiero di Graziano e dei suoi interpreti', *Studia Gratiana* 3, 1955, 193–276.

2. For fuller citation of the commentators on Gratian see my two studies: G. King, 'The Acceptance of Law by the Community: A Study in the Writings of Canonists and Theologians, 1500–1750', *The Jurist* 37, 1977, 233–365; id., *The Acceptance of Law by the Community as an Integral Element in the Formation of Canon Law: An Historical and Analytical Study*, Canon Law Studies 498, Washington 1979.

3. A point which I have argued at greater length in the studies cited in note 2 (see especially 'The Acceptance', 250–8).

4. Cited in B. Tierney, *Foundations of the Conciliar Theory*, Cambridge 1955, 81.

5. For the councils of the first millennium see especially H.-J. Sieben, *Die Konzilsidee der alten Kirche*, Paderborn 1979, and 'Episcopal Conferences in Light of Particular Councils during the First Millenium', *The Jurist* 48 1988 30–56.

6. Sieben, 'Particular Councils' (n. 5), 33.

7. B. Tierney, 'The Idea of Representation in the Medieval Councils of the West', *Concilium* 167, 1983, 27.

8. For discussion of these matters we continue to be indebted to Brian Tierney's 1955 work, *Foundations of the Conciliar Theory*.

9. Tierney, *Foundations*, 177.

10. Tierney, *Foundations*, 149.

11. Tierney, *Foundations*, 141–149.

12. R. Lawrence, 'The Building of Consensus: The Conciliar Rules of Procedure and the Evolution of *Dei Verbum*', *The Jurist* 46, 1986, 474–510.

Democracy in the Jesuit Order?

Peter J. Huizing

Can anything like democracy exist in 'the Pope's army' or fit in with the lament of the pious Lucien Laberthonnière: 'Constantine made the church an imperial empire, St Thomas made it a system and Ignatius made it a police state?' Especially when Ignatius in his letter on obedience compares this virtue with the availability of a body? That was an idea from Francis of Assisi, found in his life by Bonaventure, but . . . what still remains of democracy after that?

What in fact is 'democracy'? The word means 'rule by the people', as opposed to monarchy, oligarchy and aristocracy. That is political democracy, a model of government, directly active only in a popular referendum on government decisions, and indirectly active in the election of members of a government. We know well enough what sometimes happens to the rights and interests of 'subjects' in so-called democratic states. Moreover social democracy in which these rights and interests are respected and protected is of real importance; this protection is what any political government needs to offer. Do Jesuits live in such a democracy?

While they were still students in Paris, on 15 August 1534 Ignatius and his friends pledged themselves to live in poverty and unmarried in the service of God and their fellow men and women, and after their studies they asked the pope's permission to settle in Jerusalem. When that permission was not granted, they put themselves at his disposal. On their arrival in Rome the pope gave them different tasks. They called themselves '*Societas Iesu*', which is best rendered 'company of Jesus', something which was still a free association. Only after long discussion of the pros and cons did they decide in 1539 to form an order under the rule of a single head, because that would be much more efficient for their common calling; for 'in all well-organized communities or congregations there must be, besides the persons who take care of the particular goals, one or several whose proper duty it is to attend to the universal good' (719). In 1540 and 1550 the *Formulae Instituti*, the rules of the order, were approved by popes Paul III and Julius III. The order's own form of government is primarily contained in the Constitutions, on which Ignatius and his helpers worked from 1540 to his death in 1556.[1]

The purpose and structure of the Constitutions

'The purpose of the Constitutions is to aid the body of the Society as a whole and also its individual members toward their preservation and development for the divine glory and the good of the universal Church. Therefore these Constitutions in addition to the fact that they in their entirety and each one of them should be conducive to this purpose stated, should have three characteristics . . .' (136). How is the general interest of the order related to that of its members? 'In the order of our intention, the consideration which comes first and has more weight is that about the body of the Society taken as a whole; for its union, good government, and preservation in well-being for the greater divine glory are what is chiefly sought. Nevertheless, this body is composed of its members, and in the order of execution, that which takes place first is what pertains to the individual members . . .' (135).

The first six parts are about 'individual members': admission to the probationary period; dismissal during the probationary period; formation during the probationary period; then pastoral and academic formation; universities of the order; acceptance into the order; personal behaviour. Then follow part 7, distributing the members over the Lord's vineyard, and 8, their unity both with their head and with one another. Only then do we have part 9, the head of the order and the government which comes down from the head, and 10, the prosperity and spread of the whole order – with the typical conclusion that it is important to take account of the health of individual persons, that all take it upon themselves to live in accordance with the constitutions, and that care must be taken that houses and colleges are established in places where the air is pure and healthy (826–7).

Obedience to the pope

Part 7 begins with the missions of the pope, as a representative of Jesus, who is the most important. The fourth vow binds members to 'special obedience to the sovereign pontiff in regard to missions' (527, 529); this obedience is to be shown without asking for money for travel or making excuses for not going to the appointed place, among believers or unbelievers, for causes which are to the glory of God and the flourishing of

Christian worship, and in a way that in the pope's judgment contributes to the greater service of God and of the pope and his Curia. The mission can and must be explained by the prelate or another through whom the pope communicates his task; the explanation is to comprise what the mission involves, what the pope has in mind by it and what result is expected from it; how he envisaged the journey and the stay, whether those concerned are to live on alms or in another way. And this is to be written down. Then the task can be carried out all the more precisely (609–613). Leaders or others may try directly or indirectly to make the pope take their own preferences into account.

Nevertheless, sometimes the pope could give a mission in which he was not well up in the situation. Then the General would have to inform him, but otherwise leave the matter to him. Should another member of the order get such a mission, which might not be in the service of God or the general interests of the order, his superior could inform the pope through the General or his staff. Anyone who did not find the hoped-for fruit through the place assigned by the pope could himself go further in search of the glory of God and human salvation. Anyone who had to stay a long time in the appointed places could himself undertake initiatives of which good results were expected. Without neglecting their task for other work, however good, those on missions had to see what they could apply themselves to next and not lose a single opportunity which God offered them.

Although these guidelines come from a world which is so different from that of today, they seek an honest obedience which sees that even papal missions cannot go against the mission of the order. Moreover, no matter how convinced Ignatius was of the urgent need to reform the papacy and its Curia, even stronger was his belief in the essential need for the unity of the church with its head appointed by Jesus, and its authority as the task of preserving and protecting the unity of believers and local communities.

The General Congregation

Chapter 8 is not about government but about 'what helps towards uniting the distant members with their head and among themselves'; chapter 1 is about 'what can aid the union of hearts', chapters 2–7 are about the General Congregation, 'what helps towards the union of person in congregations or chapters' and at the same time its supreme organ of authority. This assembly is held for the choice of the General, and otherwise only for matters of great and abiding general importance. It is summoned by the representative of a General who has died or resigned, otherwise by the

General. Every three years the General, his closest colleagues and representatives from around eighty-four provinces, the provincial heads or appointed delegates by rotation, hold a meeting which among other things considers and decides whether or not there is a need for a General Congregation.

The General and his closest colleagues take part in the General Congregation, with one delegate each from provinces with less than 0.5% of the total number of members and between two and seven delegates from the others, depending on the number of their members. The delegates are elected by the provincial assemblies. Provincials, the local heads nominated by the General, the province procurator and the chosen members, take part in these. Those who have been members for more than five years have an active right to vote, and those who have been members for more than eight years have a passive right to vote. Of those who have not yet finished their formation, at least one and at most five members can take part. In the spirit of this tendency to the unity and integration of all members in the life of the order, the General must see that during the studies which are necessary arrangements are made about participation in the General Congregation, especially of the lay brothers who have been trained.

Thus the members of the provinces have a decisive influence on the convening of the provincial and general congregations. Here all members have the right to communicate possible wishes in the interest of the order to the provincial congregation, through this also to the General Congregation, and even, if necessary, directly to the General Congregation. Moreover the participants can also make known to the General Congregation other standpoints which have been arrived at in their provincial congregations. These too have a right to attention.

The position of the General

At first sight the General indeed has an exceptionally concentrated power of government. Apart from his four general assistants and his personal counsellor, who are appointed by the General Congregation, he nominates colleagues, provincial superiors and local superiors whose nomination is reserved for him – though this must remain limited to posts of general importance. Provincial superiors can only nominate local superiors with his approval, and that also applies to all their major decisions, like the establishment and disbanding of houses, colleges and universities. The General is the only superior to be nominated for life; provincial superiors are nominated for six and local overseers for three years, but on the whole, unless their appointment is terminated, the latter usually also serve for a maximum of six years; however, apart from the General, none of the other superiors can remain too long without an interruption in their governing functions. Within the norms laid down by the Constitutions and the general congregations, the General has legislative power for the whole order, and provincial superiors for their provinces only with his consent. In short, all the posts of authority within the order are regarded as participating in that of the General. Viewed only from this aspect, in fact a tendency can arise to term his position that of a 'general' or a 'black pope'.

But there is also another side. First of all it is constantly stressed that he has to exercise his office in the service of God for the wellbeing of his order, its members and the people for whom it works, in regular consultation with his staff and in contact with the provinces, which are very different, especially in the assemblies of provincials and elected delegates. In this connection the regulations about 'the authority of provident care which the Society should exercise in regard to the Superior General' are the most significant.

He must accept the advice of his assistants over his way of life, in terms of clothing, diet, personal responsibilities, and over his health, so that he does not take on too much work himself or live too strictly. On his secretariat the Constitutions state: 'The general obviously ought to have one person who ordinarily accompanies him and should be his memory and hands for everything which he must write and handle, and finally for all the affairs of his office. This person should take on the general's own person and imagine that he carries on his own shoulders the general's whole burden (except for his authority)' (800). His counsellor has the care of his personal life and work and can also be his confessor. Unless the pope imposes it on him by virtue of his vow, thus without sin, he cannot accept any church dignity as a result of which he would have to lay down his own office.

If the majority of his general assistants are convinced that because of age, sickness or another serious cause the General is no longer in a position to exercise his office and thus has to resign, they must communicate this to him through his counsellors. Any further procedure depends on his assent. If after consultation, again from all the provinces, the majority also recognize the need, a Vicar General must replace him. Finally, should the General ever offend through any scandalous be- haviour, and this is accepted by the majority of the general assistants, then they themselves must summon a General Congregation; should what has happened be generally acknowledged, then the provincial superiors must consult and agree without waiting for appeal from the assistants. Here, too, what applies to all those in authority in the order also applies, namely that power has been given to them to do good, as far as possible, but without misusing it; in that case the whole body has to meet together.

The preservation of the body (292–306)

Finally, after the above-mentioned rules about 'political democracy', there is at least one about 'social democracy': the concern of those in authority for the health and physical strength of the members. Account must be taken of each individual in accordance with his needs, depending on whether anyone is injured in any way, whether they have any problems about food, clothing, housing, sleep, work, etc. More than during the probationary period care must be taken to see that students have sensible and appropriate clothing, for they have to study and also have fees for lectures. Above all in the summer, no hard physical work must be done for an hour or two after the midday meal. Some form of physical exercise is recommended which benefits body and spirit, even for those engaged in intellectual work. In the houses, able-bodied members with stamina must care for the sick, and be appointed sacristans and receptionists. As many tasks as possible such as being in charge of water, timber and suchlike, must be carried out by members of the order.

One could point to more regulations for the sharing of labour and respect for personal rights and interests, and not just in this order, and their connection with the spirituality, aims and scope of religious communities and indeed with church communities and church government. However, although this is an important issue, to embark on it would take us too far afield.

Translated by John Bowden

Notes

1. *Societatis Iesu Constitutiones et Epitome Instituti*, Rome 1962; D. van den Akker, P. Begheyn, J. van Hijst, C. Verhaak, *Konstituties van de Sociëteit van Jezus. Proeve van een vertaling*, Nijmegen 1966–67; Johannes G. Gerhartz, *Compendium Practicum iuris Societatis Iesus*, secunda editio recognita, Rome 1986; *Dekreten van de 31ste Generale Congregatie 1965–1966*, The Hague 1967; *Decreta Congregationis Generalis XXXII; a restituta Societate XIII. Annis 1974–1975*, Rome 1975; *Documenten van de dreiendertigste Algemene Congregatie van de Sociëteit van Jezus (1 September–25 Oktober 1983)*, Brussels and The Hague 1984; *Collectio decretorum Congregationum Generalium Societatis Iesu*, tertia editio, Rome 1977; George E. Ganss SJ, *The Constitutions of the Society of Jesus. Translated with an Introduction and a Commentary*, St Louis 1970; Dominique Bertrand, SJ, *Un corps pour l'esprit*.

Essai sur l'expérience communautaire selon les Constitutions de la Compagnie de Jesus, Paris 1974; Thomas E. Clancy SJ, *An Introduction to Jesuit life. The Constitutions and History through 435 Years*, St Louis 1976; Philip Debruyne SJ (ed.), *Een weg naar God. Drie documenten uit de beginjaren van de jezuïtenorde*, Mechelen-Nijmegen 1989; *Jesuit sein heute. Formel des Instituts. Satzungen, Dekrete der Gesellschaft Jesu. Ein Auswahl*, Rome 1991.

Democracy in Dominican Government

Patricia Walter, OP

I. Historical context

The twelfth to the fourteenth centuries were a time of ferment in canon law as that law grappled with the practical and theoretical issues raised by the appearance of new forms of organization such as guilds, confraternities and universities. The corporation theory and law which developed by the middle of the thirteenth century held 'that authority in a corporation was not concentrated in the head alone but resided in all the members; and as a practical consequence it followed that the prelate could not act without consent of the members in the more important matters affecting the well-being of the whole corporation'.[1] This idea was expressed in the principle: 'what affects everyone should be treated and approved by everyone'. The principle was gradually extended from matters involving bishops and the canons of their cathedral chapters to the relationship between the pope and the college of cardinals and finally to the relationship between the pope and the whole church. Such a theory ran counter to the claims of the Decretalists and Innocent IV that the pope possessed a *plenitudo potestatis* directly from God, that he was absolutely sovereign in the church and above all human law. The debates during these centuries sound familiar; among the contentious issues were the origin of ecclesial authority, the relationship between the head and members of a group, what if any limitations existed to the authority of the head, the significance of election and of ecclesial groups.

The Dominican Order came into being during this period. In 1215, Dominic sought confirmation of an Order of Preachers from Innocent III. This was a necessary move, for the sole *ordo praedicatorum* until that time was the bishops. The Lateran council, then in session, had addressed the issue of unauthorized preaching. It would also forbid the formation of new religious orders. Innocent therefore told Dominic to return to his companions in Toulouse and to decide unanimously on an existing rule. In 1216, the small band adopted the rule of St Augustine and developed a customary, based on that of the Premonstratensians, to regulate their life in community together. These men became canons regular, members of a community attached to the church of St Romanus. They shared with Dominic a commitment to preaching the gospel in a land riddled with heresy. They assumed that they would go out from this community, and other communities attached to churches in the area, to conduct preaching tours. Unlike other groups of canons, stability was ensured not by connection with a place but by a vow of obedience to Dominic.

Dominic returned to Rome and received confirmation of his community in December 1216. A bull issued a month later explicitly confirmed the mission of the Order as an Order of Preachers. Dominic was recognized as the head or prior of the Order. While still in Rome, however, Dominic had a vision of his band being scattered throughout the world. He returned to Toulouse, delighting his comrades with the news that their mission had been confirmed and stunning them with his decision to send members of the fledgling community across Europe. Dominic continued to obtain papal bulls to establish the legitimacy of his Order in new territories. These bulls acknowledged Dominic's authority and the mission of the Order. At no time, however, was the legislation of the Order submitted for approbation. So Simon Tugwell observes, '[Dominic's] Order is constituted by its ecclesiastical mandate to preach, not by its mode of religious life or monastic organization'.[2]

By the end of 1219, there were priories of Dominicans in France, Italy, Spain and Germany. At this point, Dominic decided to convene a general chapter. The Preachers had a confirmed mission, the effective authority of Dominic and the priors he had appointed, and documents detailing community life. However, in the light of the rapid growth of the Order and Dominic's weakening health, they needed to develop a government structure which would facilitate their mission and ensure unity and continuity. The chapter convened in Bologna, home of the University of Bologna and its renowned faculty of canon law, in May 1220. The capitulars included representatives from all the foundations; among them were two doctors of canon law at the university. Dominic again surprised his brothers by tendering his resignation. While they rejected his resignation, they agreed to elect four diffinitors to preside over the chapter. This chapter fashioned the basic legislation for Dominican government. In

1221, the chapter again met at Bologna and expanded its legislation by developing intermediate, provincial structures.

II. Principles of Dominican government

The government designed collegially in Bologna has three basic elements: 'a deliberative assembly, a personal authority, an electoral body'.[3] Every level has its legitimate autonomy. The professed members of a priory form a conventual chapter, which elects its *prior* (not *abbot* or *superior*), and mutually determines certain matters pertaining to common life and ministry. The conventual chapters also elect their representatives to the provincial chapters.

In addition to electing priors provincial and representatives to the general chapters, provincial chapters address matters of concern at the regional level. They may evaluate the administration of local priories and the province, make decisions concerning present problems, and chart future directions.

The general chapter has full power over any issues of government and administration as well as responsibility for directing the Order's life in mission. When it is in session, this body has supreme executive, legislative and judicial authority. It is the only body which can make changes in the Constitutions and enact other legislation. It can also deal with breaches of religious discipline and remove officials, including the Master, from office. As part of a unique system of checks and balances, the Constitutions drawn up at Bologna provided for two successive chapters composed of an elected representative from each province, followed by a chapter consisting of all the provincials. In 1228, the general chapter decreed that any new legislation must be approved by three successive chapters, thus ensuring that the legislation was necessary for the common good.

The Bologna chapters described the rights of the general chapter; aside from acknowledging the possibility of excesses, they made no legislation concerning the authority of the Master. Between chapters, the Master of the Order has full authority as head of the Order. This authority is linked with the fact that Dominicans are incorporated into the Order through profession of one vow: obedience to the Master.

The Master of the Order is thus a sign and principle of unity for a mobile and far-flung apostolic community. He exercises his authority within the constitutional limits established by the community through its chapters. He has supreme executive authority; he is not the executive secretary of the general chapter. His position also differs from that of heads of state in governments which have a legislative body continuously in session. The

Master also has judicial authority. As head of an exempt clerical order, the Master has as well the ecclesiastical power of jurisdiction. The Master confirms the election of provincials, who in turn confirm the elections of priors. Provincials function like the Master in their own territory. Although officials may not legislate, they have broad powers of dispensation for the sake of the mission. This power of dispensation insures flexibility and adaptability.

The government of communities of Dominican women incorporates these basic principles and structures. Members are incorporated into the community through profession of obedience to the Prioress of the monastery or congregation. The Prioress has full executive authority within the group. Legislation and elections occur in chapters. Larger congregations do have intermediate provincial structures. Dominican monasteries and congregations are autonomous; the Master is simply recognized as head of the Order. The constitutional legislation of communities of Dominican women must, however, be approved by the Congregation for Institutes of Consecrated Life and for Societies of Apostolic Life.

Within the communion of members, authority is exercised in various ways. It functions within stable offices and participative structures; it is expressed through elections and corporate decisions as well as through persons or groups charged with responsibilities for particular dimensions of the common mission. Dominican government thus has a balance of corporate decision-making and authority vested in elected officials. Significant decisions are made consensually, either by chapters or by the elected officials and their councils, respecting the principle of subsidiarity.

Accountability and co-responsibility are built into the system. Elected officials are accountable to the bodies which elected them as well as to officials and chapters with more extensive authority. Members are accountable to the community through its representative bodies and the elected officials. All are responsible for the mission of the Order. There is a basic equality among all members, with those elected exercising authority for limited terms and then returning to their normal status.

The authority of general chapters and of the Master of the Order (or Prioress of the Congregation) provides the necessary centralization: the authority of provincial and conventual chapters and their elected officials ensures subsidiarity. Elected officials exercise their authority within the framework of the Constitutions, the corporate document of the group. The legislative power of chapters is accompanied by the ability of officials to give dispensations. Thus, the government structure has a remarkable system of checks and balances, the authority necessary to preserve unity and promote the mission, and the capacity for adaptation and flexibility.

III. Reflections on democracy in Dominican government

Dominic drew his inspiration for the Order of Preachers from the missionary mandate of Jesus to the apostles (Matt. 28. 18–20), from the description of the apostolic community given in Acts 2, and from his own experience. This inspiration took flesh through the creative modification of existing practices and the utilization of contemporary theories. Thus Dominican government is fundamentally an expression of evangelical principles as they were interpreted by eminent theologians and canon lawyers in a time of transition from feudalism to corporate theory. As Vincent de Couesnongle, a former Master of the Order, observes:

> The Order is something new, something in line with the Gospel, and therefore with the Kingdom of God which makes us all brothers. To set up this type of life, recourse was had to certain structures which, in political science, are called democratic, where sovereignty belongs to the whole group of citizens.[4]

Such structures, de Couesnongle continues, 'give institutional shape' to the community of brothers and/or sisters envisioned by Jesus (Matt. 23.8). This vision must modify any form of government existing within the church.

Dominican government is certainly democratic or participative. However, the origin of its authority is clearly not mere political will, nor is its focus organizational efficiency. It is connected with the Dominican charism, which is a specification of the common ecclesial mission and which has been affirmed by the church through the recognition of the community as an Order of *Preachers*. The charism entails basic rights and duties. Adult men and women who have freely responded to this gift of the Spirit share responsibility for the life of the community in mission. Through profession of the vow of obedience, Dominican women and men commit themselves to discover and incarnate God's saving will as members of a specific historical community. Participation in Dominican government is thus participation in a common search for truth. So de Couesnongle notes that while a democracy may be satisfied with a rule of the majority, the structures of Dominican life are intended to bring about, in dialogical fashion, virtual unanimity in the search for God's will and corporate responsibility in responding to that will.

As Gadamer has pointed out, the discovery of truth both presumes and fashions community. The dialogical pursuit of truth creates a common understanding, a knowledge which shapes human beings and their praxis. It forms women and men capable of full freedom and full citizenship. Dominicans prepare for and accompany this communal search for truth by careful programmes of formation as well as continual individual and communal prayer and study. Such qualities and activities are indispensable to the achievement of the Order's primary purpose, a life of evangelical witness for the sake of apostolic preaching.

Religious life is a charism, a divine gift to and for the whole church. As a way of life publicly recognized by the church, it is an institutionalized charism. The freely chosen, distinctively communal dimension of religious life has been expressed in a marvellous diversity of structures. Thus, the experience of religious institutes has yielded a practical knowledge which may provide insight into the church's understanding of itself as a *communio*, a community existing in and through the unity of the Trinity and participating in the mission of reconciliation. The experience of Dominicans, an ecclesial 'experiment' enduring for nearly eight hundred years, may well be of help as the church continues to renew its structures to reflect the presence of the risen Christ in the Spirit within the whole community.

Notes

1. B. Tierney, *Foundations of the Conciliar Theory*, Cambridge 1955, 117.
2. S. Tugwell, *The Way of the Preacher*, Springfield, Ill. and London 1979, 19.
3. P. Mandonnet, *St Dominic and His Work*, St Louis and London 1944, 321.
4. V. de Couesnongle, *Confidence for the Future*, Dublin 1982, 112.

Synodality in the Eastern Catholic Churches according to the New Code

George Nedungatt SJ

Since democracy embodies values much appreciated in society today, the question may be asked: Is the new *Code of Canons of the Eastern Churches*[1] democratic? The answer may be yes or no or both, depending on the meaning attached to democracy. Concepts taken from one subject like politics or civil law may not always apply in the same sense in ecclesiology or canon law. If democracy means universal suffrage, parliamentary representation and the choice of government by majority vote, then the new Eastern code is not democratic. But these are but democratic tools, whose aim is ultimately consultation and power-sharing for the common good. This goal and purpose of democracy is substantially preserved in the Eastern principle of synodality. A closer look at it in the modern context can be rewarding.

In the West hierarchy has come to be associated with church monarchy set at the antipodes of democracy. In the East, synodality achieves a synthesis of the monarchic and the democratic principles in an equilibrium that avoids the defects and weaknesses both have in their extremes or isolation. In this sense Eastern synodality is a happy church marriage between monarchy and democracy.[2] This is not to say that the Eastern hierarchy is synodal right through: there are monarchic church structures also in the East, where – to return to the metaphor – monarchy remains celibate, unaffected by democracy., The new Eastern Code of the Catholic Church needs to be studied not only in comparison with its Latin counterpart (CIC) but also examining the wellsprings of the Eastern synodal tradition it has drawn on. The synodal structure is, according to oriental theology, both the exigency of communion and the expression of unity of the church and of the churches.[3] And the milestones of the ancient Oriental canonical tradition are:[4] canon 34 of the Apostles, Nicaea I (325)

c. 4; Synod of Antioch (341) c. 9; Constantinople I (381) cc. 2, 6; Chalcedon (451) cc. 9, 19, etc.[5] Though apocryphal like the Apostles' Creed, Canon 34 of the Apostles has guided all oriental tradition like a fixed star.

Before we proceed we need to settle on a few abbreviations:

CIC	*Codex Iuris Canonici 1983*
CCEO	*Codex Canonum Ecclesiarum Orientalium*
LEF	*Lex Ecclesiae Fundamentalis*
PCCICOR	Pontificia Commissio Codicis Iuris Canonici Orientalis Recognoscendo
Nuntia	(=Organ of PCCICOR) nn. 1–31 (1975–1990).

The basic difference between the Eastern and the Western codes lies in their ecclesiological substratum. Roman Catholic or Western ecclesiology (heir to the mediaeval dialectics between *imperium et sacerdotium*, the two parallel and universal powers of emperor and pope) has a two-tier structure and sees the hierarchical unity of the church at two levels: at the level of the *universal church* in the person of the pope and at the level of the diocese (*particular* church) in the person of the diocesan bishop. If we prescind for a moment from the ecumenical councils, which are after all rare events in the juridical life of the church, this Western model is monarchic[6] in both the tiers: all powers – legislative, executive or administrative, and judicial – are cumulated in the pope (CIC c. 331) or in the bishop (c. 391).

Eastern Catholic ecclesiology posits a three-tier structure, which includes an intermediate level between the aforementioned two.[7] This structure is not obvious from *CCEO* with its division into thirty titles. The peculiarity of the intermediate tier is that it is non-monarchic in structure, unlike the other two. And it is synodal in character. The Eastern Orthodox ecclesiology does not see the supreme authority as monarchic but as synodal.

The following comparative table can serve to bring out the similarities and differences in the hierarchical structure posited by the three ecclesiologies, the Orthodox (A), the Eastern Catholic (B) and the Western Catholic (C).

Tier	Orthodox A	Eastern Catholic B	Western Catholic C
1. universal	synodal	monarchic	monarchic
2. intermediate	synodal	synodal	. . .
3. eparchial or diocesan	monarchic	monarchic	monarchic

In this prospectus, which is rather formal and abstract, the least monarchic (or most 'democratic') is A, which contrasts most with C (1, 3), while B is intermediary. Dealing only with this last model (B) here, we shall in the first part of our study examine in some detail the intermediate level (2), where church government is strictly synodal. And then in a second part, by way of contrast and complementarity, we shall glance briefly at the two monarchic structures (1 and 3), where however elements of consultation and participation are not lacking.

To study synodality in the Eastern Catholic churches we have first to take a look at the ecclesiastical hierarchy as set forth in the new code, which envisages, according to C. 174, the following four types of *churches sui iuris*,[8] namely:

1. Patriarchal church (*CCEO*, cc. 55–150);
2. Major archiepiscopal church (cc. 151–154);
3. Metropolitan church *sui iuris* (cc. 155–173);
4. 'Remainder churches' (cc. 174–176).[9]

This fourfold division also marks four grades of churches on a descending scale of ecclesial autonomy from a canonical standpoint. Each of these grades of churches is headed by a single hierarch:[10] (*a*) patriarch, (*b*) major archbishop, (*c*) metropolitan, (*d*) bishop or exarch or apostolic vicar, etc. who heads a diocese, exarchate, etc., which is not incorporated in any of the preceding three churches. These hierarchs each embody and symbolize the unity of the church which he represents juridically (*personam gerit*).

I. Synodal structures

1. First grade: patriarchal churches
The word 'patriarchal' in law is free of the sinister notions associated with it in feminist literature ('patriarchal culture'). The patriarch of an Eastern Catholic church does not have the fullness of power in his church. Broadly speaking, according to *CCEO*, of the three powers – legislative, executive, judicial – he has only one, namely the second. He can exercise this power in several cases only after getting the consent or the advice of a synod and/or of the Roman See. Critics have rated differently this division of power in the patriarchal church. One extreme view is that the patriarch has been reduced to an inferior status like a Latin archbishop. The opposite extreme view holds that he has been exalted to a junior pope. These contrasting opinions can be a sign that the right equilibrium has been struck by the code.[11]

A decrease of patriarchal powers in the code in favour of the synods will be greeted as a move in the direction of 'democracy' by those who rate as too absolutist ('Pharaonic') the mediaeval patriarchal model. In the Middle Ages in certain Eastern churches powers got concentrated in the patriarch, who was ecclesiastical and civil head of a minority Christian community living mostly in a hostile milieu. Most of the ancient synodal powers were gradually transferred to the patriarch, and the synod became almost nominal. *CCEO* does not legislate for such abnormal conditions, but restores the ancient synodal structure, updating it in the light of the ecclesiology of Vatican II. On many counts this turns out to be agreeable also to the modern democratic outlook.[12] Let us now look at certain details of the division of power in *CCEO*.

The *legislative* power resides exclusively in the episcopal synod of the patriarchal church,[13] which is made up of all the bishops of that church (c. 102) and is the expression of their co-responsibility. Unlike the pope, who can enact laws *motu proprio*, all by himself, the patriarch by himself is no legislator. He is a legislator only as part of the episcopal synod, of which he is the statutory president. Using an analogy, we can say that the episcopal synod is, in some respects, like the parliament of a constitutional democracy. It exercises its legislative power within the limits of common law, that is the law common to all the oriental churches or to the universal church (c. 1493 § 1). The binding force of its laws is limited to the territory of the patriarchal church unless laws are approved by the Roman See or unless they are liturgical laws. All the laws enacted by the episcopal synod are to be communicated to the pope for information, but not for approval or confirmation (c. 111 § 3) unless they are laws involving liturgical reform. In this latter case, the laws as well as the liturgical texts are to be submitted for prior review by the Roman See (c. 657 § 1). While the authority of the bishops in the Latin church to teach as episcopal conference has been disputed, the authority of the episcopal synods of patriarchal churches (and of the councils of hierarchs of metropolitan churches (*sui iuris*: see below) to teach, is clearly stated (c. 605).

The episcopal synod has also *judicial* powers, which are exercised directly or indirectly. The synod itself is the highest tribunal of the patriarchal church. It appoints a tribunal of three bishops with power to adjudge cases, including those against bishops or eparchies of the patriarchal church in contentious trials. Appeal from this tribunal is to the synod itself (c. 1062), as to a high court. An example: a parish priest is served an order of transfer by his bishop. If he feels he is wronged thereby (cf. cc. 1397–1400), he can contest the justice of the transfer before the above-mentioned tribunal. In the Latin church, in which there is no real superepiscopal authority below the pope, such a case against one's bishop will have to be taken to Rome and filed before the Roman Rota (*CIC* c. 1405 § 3 1°; *Pastor Bonus*, 129). In a patriarchal church the same case (if it is not resolved administratively by the metropolitan or the patriarch) can be filed locally, investigated more easily and judged more rapidly and with greater economy. These facilities may cause, as a by-product, an increase in local litigations. But that is the price we have to pay as human beings to obtain the advantages of justice. The alternative may be a peace without justice, because people do not or cannot take their cases abroad out of ignorance or despair.

The patriarchal church is judicially self-sufficient, so that appeals in the second or the third grades can also be heard by the patriarchal tribunal using a system of rotation of judges (c. 1063 § 3). This forestalls the need, for example, to send marriage cases to Rome, except for the dissolution of non-consummated marriages (c. 862). This self-sufficiency is but an application of the conciliar declaration that 'patriarchs with their synods are the highest authority for all business of the patriarchate' (OE 9). This provision, however, does not deny the primatial role of the Roman See, to which appeal or recourse is always possible at any stage of the trial (c. 1059). The Roman primacy has some analogy with the supreme court in a democratic state. Any case against the patriarch himself or a criminal case against bishops has to be filed before the pope (c. 1060) and not before the episcopal synod as in the ancient oriental tradition. This provision is an updating and not a betrayal of tradition: it should forestall internal hierarchical rifts in a patriarchal church and contribute to the very honour of the hierarchs.[14] The primatial see also keeps vigilance over the judiciary in all the Eastern Catholic Churches, even as in the Latin Church, through the Signatura Apostolica.[15]

While the legislative and the judicial powers are invested in the episcopal synod, the executive or *administrative power* is mostly in the hands of the patriarch (c. 110 § 4). He is elected for life by the episcopal synod (c. 63). He has vast powers of administration. While CIC reserves to Rome the creation of new dioceses (c. 373) and the appointment of bishops (c. 377 § 1), these and even more important matters like the erection of ecclesiastical provinces and the nomination and the transfer of metropolitans in CCEO (cc 85, 86) come under the competence of the patriarch. Here is the full text of c. 85:

§ 1. For a grave reason, with the consent of the Synod of Bishops and after consulting the Apostolic See, the patriarch can erect provinces and eparchies, modify their boundaries, unite, divide, or suppress them, change their hierarchical grade and transfer the episcopal see.

§ 2. The patriarch is competent with the consent of the Episcopal Synod of the Patriarchal Church:

1° to give to an eparchial bishop a coadjutor bishop or an auxiliary bishop, observing cc. 181 § 1, 182–187 and 212.

2° for a grave reason to transfer a metropolitan or an eparchial or titular bishop to another metropolitan, eparchial or titular see; in case of refusal, the Synod of Bishops is to resolve the matter or defer it to the Roman Pontiff.

§ 3. The patriarch can erect, change or suppress exarchies with the consent of the Permanent Synod.

§ 4. The patriarch is to notify the Apostolic See of these decisions as soon as possible.

The apostolic see of Rome is to be consulted prior to the execution of the synodal decision to erect, modify or suppress eparchies and provinces. In fact all important decisions have to be communicated to it. New bishops for sees within the territorial limits of the patriarchal church[16] are elected by the synod of bishops from a list of candidates it has approved and for which the prior consent of the pope has been obtained (cc. 182, 183); bishops for sees outside the territorial limits are nominated by Rome, but the synod can present a list of three candidates (c. 149). In c. 85 § 3 cited above we met with another synod called the permanent synod, to which we shall return shortly.

Let us take three other examples which illustrate various degrees of sharing of authority and responsibility: the erection or establishment 1. of an intereparchial seminary, 2. of a Catholic university, 3. of an ecclesiastical university. In the first case, the patriarch must get the consent of the synod of bishops (c. 334); in the second case he must also consult the apostolic see of Rome (c. 642); in the third case he has to act together with that See (*una cum Sede Apostolica* c. 649). Where the patriarch cannot act alone or *motu proprio* but needs the consent of the episcopal synod, the synod may be said to share in the administrative powers of the patriarch, who is 'the highest administrative authority' in his church (cc. 542, 649).

Occasionally the synod as such is the proper subject of administrative acts, as for example in issuing a plan of clerical formation (c. 330) or catechetical directories and catechisms for use in the whole patriarchal church (c. 621). These administrative acts, which are fully and directly synodal, may be initiated as it were from the floor, whereas for the former kind it is normal for the initiative to come from the patriarch himself. In case he fails to do so, his hand can be forced by one third of the synod members who jointly ask for the convocation of the synod (c. 106 § 1 3°).

The episcopal synod comprising all the bishops is naturally too unwieldy to convoke frequently. The patriarch normally convokes it as need arises (c. 103). The ordinary administration and urgent business cannot wait for these expensive and infrequent sessions. To expedite such matters law provides for another organ called the permanent synod.[17] This is a minor synod and forms part of the patriarchal curia. It consists of five bishops in all including the patriarch, who is its president; three are elected by the episcopal synod (cc. 114–120). So, the permanent synod is a representative body: it represents the larger episcopal synod and through it the whole patriarchal church. It thus provides for the needed check and balance between the monarchic and the democratic principles. The patriarch needs the consent of the permanent synod for certain administrative acts like convoking the episcopal synod (c. 106 § 1 2°) or accepting the resignation of a bishop (c. 210 § 3). So too, he must ask its counsel to give an authentic interpretation of laws enacted by the episcopal synod, an interpretation that will be valid till the next episcopal synod (c. 112 § 2), which may then confirm or revoke it. The patriarch needs the consent of the permanent synod in about twenty five cases in all and its counsel or advice in about fifteen others.

Some administrative acts of less importance are within the competence of the patriarch himself, who need not refer to any of the two foregoing synods: for example, to dispense from impediments to sacred orders which are beyond a bishop to dispense from (c. 767) or to hear the recourse of a religious against his or her dismissal (c. 501 § 3, 553).

Such, briefly, is the power distribution enacted by CCEO for the patriarchal churches. These churches thus possess considerable autonomy vis-à-vis the central or supreme authority of the Roman See. They are invested with the highest grade of ecclesial autonomy, having various legislative, judicial and administrative organs in sharp contrast to the regional or national units of the Latin Church, presided over by episcopal conferences having little powers of self-determination.

The powers of a patriarchal church in the Catholic communion can be compared to those of autocephalous Orthodox churches.[18] The chief difference is that while the Orthodox see the supreme church authority as vested only in the ecumenical council, the Catholics recognize it also in the Roman Pontiff. In other words, for a Catholic the supreme authority is both synodal and monarchic, for an Orthodox it is only synodal.[19]

The impression created by the patriarchal church so far is, however, that of a *clerical* church. It is synodal, but is it not 'aristocratically' or 'oligarchically' clerical? What is the place of the laity in the power structure of the patriarchal church? The lay people do not have much of a place in that structure. The laity have seats in the patriarchal convocation (cc. 140–145), which is but a consultative organ. It consists of the whole hierarchy and a cross section of the church. At least two lay people from each eparchy have to be 'designated in the manner determined by the eparchial bishop' (c. 143 6°). That need not mean 'democratic' election; they could be nominated. The number two may be increased by the eparchial bishop, who determines also the manner of designating the representatives of the clergy and the religious (c. 143 § 1 6°). The patriarchal convocation is a new creation of CCEO. Its counterpart in the Latin Church in the postconciliar era would be the All-India Seminar (1969), the Pastoral Council (Netherlands, 1970), the *Gemeinsame Synode* (West Germany, 1971–1975), the National Pastoral Congress (England and Wales, 1980). Unlike these and unlike the eparchial convocation (see below eparchial structure and more about the laity) the Patriarchal Convocation is to be a recurring event: it is to be held every five years, but the patriarch may convoke it oftener with the consent of the permanent synod or of the episcopal synod (c. 141).

2. Second grade: major archiepiscopal churches

Next to the patriarchal church comes the church presided over by a major archbishop – the only one in the Catholic communion today is the Ukrainian church. It too has the same structure and almost the same autonomy as that of a patriarchal church. The chief difference is that the election of the major archbishop needs to be confirmed by the pope (c. 153), while that of a patriarch is only notified, which is done traditionally also to the other patriarchs (c. 76). Secondly, a patriarch has precedence over a major archbishop.

'What is stated in common law about Patriarchal Churches or about patriarchs is applicable to Major Archiepiscopal Churches and to major archbishops as well, unless common law expressly provides otherwise or it is evident from the nature of the matter' (c. 152). In brief, what was said about the synodal system of the patriarchal church applies here as well.

3. Third grade: metropolitan churches sui iuris

In the metropolitan church *sui iuris*, which is the third rung of *sui iuris* churches, there is greater dependence on the supreme authority and consequently less ecclesial autonomy. Such a church is like an ecclesiastical province but is not part of any other *sui iuris* church like a patriarchal church. Like this, it too is a distinct church. It is the competence of the supreme church authority (in practice the pope) to erect it, determine its territory, assign its see, nominate its metropolitan, or finally if need be to suppress it (c. 155). However, the metropolitan so nominated has to ask for and obtain the pallium (cf. CIC c. 437 § 1) from the Roman Pontiff as a sign of hierarchical communion before he can perform certain major administrative acts like ordaining bishops (CCEO c. 156).

Here, too, the church government is not monarchical but synodal or conciliar. Much of the powers rests with a hierarchical organ called council of hierarchs. It is composed of all the bishops of the metropolitan church *sui iuris* (c. 164). It is convoked and presided over by the metropolitan (c. 159 2°). The legislative power rests with it, not with the metropolitan. Before promulgating the laws enacted by it he must first communicate them to the Holy See and wait to be informed in writing about their 'reception' by Rome (167 § 2). With this clause the supreme authority can block any legislation or propose or demand corrections to be introduced into laws before their promulgation. Even so, the legislative power of the council of hierarchs far outweighs that of its counterpart in the Latin Church, namely the episcopal conferences (CIC c. 455) or the particular councils (CIC c. 446).

The administrative power is divided between the metropolitan and the council of hierarchs. The metropolitan can act only with the consent of the council of hierarchs in cases where the common law commits administrative acts to the highest authority of a *sui iuris* church (CCEO c. 167 § 4). In order to avoid conflict of competence between the council and the metropolitan, the statutes of the council, which have to be framed by the council itself (and are to be transmitted to the Roman see for information, not for approval, c. 171) will have to spell out the respective areas of competence. A guideline can be found in the following ideal norm: 'In extraordinary matters or those entailing special difficulty, eparchial bishops are not to omit consulting the metropolitan nor the metropolitan the eparchial bishops' (c. 160).

This canon is a modern version of the thirty-fourth canon of the Apostles, which set the ideal of the Eastern synodal tradition. It prescribed: 'The bishops of each people (province) should recognize their primate (*prótos*) and consider him as their head; they should do nothing uncommon without his knowledge, . . . and in his turn he is not to do anything without the knowledge of all; for thus there will be concord, and God will be glorified, the Father, the Son and the Holy Spirit.' This famous canon, taken over by the Synod of Antioch in 341 (c. 9), is an ecclesial reflection of the trinitarian circuminsession, and has remained at the core of the Orthodox doctrine of synodality.[20]

The division of administrative power between the council and the metropolitan must provide for a healthy equilibrium or check and balance. This is foreseen in the code. The metropolitan can transfer, prorogate, suspend or dissolve the council (c. 159, 2°). But he cannot suspend or dissolve it indefinitely. It must be convoked 'at least once a year and whenever special circumstances require it or for the carrying out of business reserved to this council by common law or for which its consent is required' (c. 170). More precise norms of check and balance can be included in the statutes.

As regards the *judicial power*, the tribunal of the metropolitan is the second instance or appellate tribunal of the Metropolitan Church *sui iuris*, the third being the Roman See (cc. 1064, 1065). The metropolitan himself has no judiciary powers over his suffragan bishops in clear contrast to the ancient discipline. This can be seen as development of discipline and need not be regarded as infidelity to tradition.

The powers of a metropolitan church *sui iuris* and their limits are to be understood in relation to its ecclesial maturity: it is not a full-grown church like a patriarchal church but is on the way to that goal. So, while some norms regarding the patriarchs already apply to the metropolitan (cc. 172, 173 §§ 2–3), in the order of precedence he comes after the major archbishop. On the other hand he has greater powers than those of an archbishop-metropolitan who heads an ecclesiastical province in the Latin church (CIC c. 435–438). The former has the right to ordain and enthrone bishops (c. 149 1°), though neither he nor the council has the power to nominate them, which is reserved to Rome. He is to be commemorated in the liturgy after the Roman Pontiff by all his clergy including the bishops (c. 162), just as the patriarch is to be commemorated in the whole patriarchal church (91). This is not only a liturgical expression of ecclesial communion but a canonical recognition of dependence on an intermediary hierarchical superior between the bishops and the pope. Orientals attach great importance to such liturgical commemoration, so much so that its contumacious neglect can merit a punishment mounting up to major excommunication (c. 1438).

Here, too, the laity have a low profile as in the patriarchal churches. Canon 172 prescribes the creation of a consultative organ, like the patriarchal convocation (cc. 140–145).

4. Fourth grade: the remainder churches

On the fourth grade of *sui iuris* churches autonomy is minimal, in fact not greater than in any other oriental eparchy or in a Latin diocese. This grade may consist of a single diocese or its equivalent like an exarchate (in a missionary region) not forming part of any of the foregoing three grades of churches. It usually expresses the initial stage of a newly evangelized community. It is canonically erected by the pope and is immediately subject to the Holy See. Obviously, there is no question of synodality when its hierarchy consists of one hierarch only; if it consists of more than one, the particular law given to it by the supreme authority will determine if and how the hierarchs are to collaborate. Accordingly, the fourth grade of churches may be regarded as a borderline case between synodality and the monarchic principle.

II. Monarchic structures

1. Eparchial power structure

The power structure at the eparchial level in CCEO is as monarchic as it is at the diocesan level in CIC. It can be summarized briefly as follows. The eparchial bishop governs his eparchy 'as the vicar and legate of Christ. The authority, which he exercises personally in the name of Christ, is proper, ordinary, and immediate', but not full or absolute, since 'the exercise of his power is ultimately regulated and can be limited within certain bounds in view of the benefit of the Church or of the Christian faithful by the supreme authority of the Church' (c. 176; *Lumen gentium* 27). With the consent of the episcopal synod, the patriarch also can curtail the powers of the diocesan bishop by transferring part or the whole of them to a coadjutor bishop (c. 213).

The bishop governs his eparchy 'with legislative, executive, and judicial power'. He 'exercises legislative power personally; he exercises executive power either personally or through the protosyncellus or syncelli; he exercises judicial power either personally or through a judicial vicar and judges' (c. 391; cf. CIC c. 391). Thus, though all the three powers are cumulated in the bishop, he may delegate two of them, while remaining himself the sole legislator.

The different eparchial organs have no powers of their own, unless by delegation or participation. This is not altered by the fact that the bishop has sometimes to consult or obtain the consent of either the council of presbyters (cc. 264–270) or of the college of consultors (cc. 271). The patriarch and the major archbishop have a rare privilege, which has been recognized by the code: in the affairs of the eparchy which they govern, they only need to consult these organs even where the canons require consent (cc. 269 §´; 271 § 6).

'It is for the eparchical bishop alone to finalize the agenda of the eparchial convocation' (= *conventus eparchialis*, c. 240 § 1), which corresponds to the diocesan synod in the Latin church (CIC, cc. 460–468). This is the assembly of a cross section of the whole eparchy, including clergy, religious and the laity (CCEO, c. 238). 'The eparchial bishop is the sole legislator in the eparchial convocation; the other participants have only a consultative vote. He alone signs all decisions . . .' (c. 241). The same pattern holds good also for the pastoral council (cc. 272–275), which may be convoked to advise the bishop on pastoral issues.

Now the purely consultative nature of these eparchial organs may often be ineffective, as ancient wisdom knew and experience proves. What is more, the Eastern tradition is different, starting with the role of the laity in the election of bishops.[21] True, in some East European countries in the recent past, lay groups were infiltrated by 'atheistic political forces' with harm to 'the hard won freedom' of the church; and this danger did weigh heavy on PCCICOR so as to reduce the laity to a consultative voice. However, this prudence may be misplaced in a different cultural context. In the Syro-Malabar Church in India, for example, where before its three centuries of Latinization, the laity had a wider role in church government through clergy-laity collaboration in *yogam*,[22] some lay leaders, disappointed with the diminished lay role in CCEO, have challenged the new code in the civil court. To be noted is that their Orthodox lay colleagues still retain the ancient prerogatives to the point that lay power struggle sometimes brings the church to a virtual standstill.

While the laypeople are 'responsible crewmen aboard the barque of the Church rather than mere passengers' (Pope John Paul I), and *Nuntia*, the official organ of PCCICOR, had a cover picture of three ships, propelled by the common code as by a *pedalion, kormcaja, alhuda*, it turns out to be ironic that CCEO allows the lay people no access to their oars.

In CCEO, power is not only clerical but male. In the early stages of codification, steps were taken to break the monopoly of male ministry in a creative return to the origins. A canon about the deaconess was to be framed, based on 'the early canons (I Nicea c. 19, Chalcedon c. 15, Trullo c. 14, Basil C. 44)', which were found 'as relevant as ever'.[23] Disputed questions were avoided like: 1. Is it theologically correct to speak of the ordination of the deaconess? 2. Does the deaconess belong with the clergy? The solution proposed in 1980 was a title *De ministris Ecclesiae in genere* with two chapters. Chapter 1: bishops, presbyters and deacons; Chapter 2: *De aliis ministris*. Among these other ministers the deaconess could be included if she was 'instituted' (generic term in antiquity including or excluding ordination) in the various churches according to their particular law. But the project did not take off for reasons not further reported. And no enquiry seems to have been made about its mysterious disappearance, seemingly because patriarchs had other worries about the new code, which they felt did not give them enough powers.

In the meanwhile, the inter-Orthodox consultation, which took place in Rhodes from 30 October to 7 November 1988, voted to revive and update the ancient institution of the deaconess. With respect to that decision the Eastern Catholic Churches and their code now fall behind the Orthodox Churches as regards the ministry of women.

2. The supreme (or central) authority

In CCEO the canons on 'the supreme authority in the church' (title III) come from LEF through CIC except for some redactional details. Any substantial departure here would of course make it non-Catholic. Beyond dogma, the theology that undergirds title III is 'Roman' and monarchic, as this is distinguished from the non-Roman interpretation of the primacy of the pope, which is not necessarily conciliarist or Gallicanist. Now, following the Roman point of view CCEO has not, any more than Vatican II's OE itself had done, presented the Catholic position in an oriental way so as to ensure better ecumenical understanding and acceptability.[24] The thirty-fourth canon of the Apostles is not built on the 'above-below' scheme, and in fact it is this canon that gives the precise insight into the oriental approach to the relationship between the pope and the patriarchs/bishops as well as to its prototype, the relationship between Peter and the other apostles.

Here we need not analyse the canons as they are already known. But it may be of some interest to register some reaction provoked by them. Strong reserve was expressed regarding title III of CCEO on the supreme authority both in the responses to its 1986 draft and in the 1988 Plenary Assembly.[25] A reworking of it was demanded for ecumenical reasons. Though CCEO recovered largely the rights and privileges of the patriarchs from 'the period of union between East and West' (OE 9), no analogous effort was made to configure the primatial authority to the same epoch 'before the separation' (UR 14) of the East and the West. The historical research had been done:[26] theology and law had to do more work for CCEO to draw on.

CCEO, following CIC, is a 'monarchic' legislation in that it has but a single legislator, the pope. The Eastern patriarchs and other heads of the Eastern Catholic churches are not even its co-legislators. Pope John Paul II alone signed the document of promulgation on 18 October 1990 in the presence of the Eastern patriarchs attending the Synod of Bishops in

Rome. So, CCEO too has the same single 'monarchic' legislator as CIC. Though it is the fruit of widespread consultation, just like CIC, and to a great extent the application of the conciliar decrees, it is strictly not a collegial, much less 'democratic', legislation.

Many Orientals see this monarchical character of the new code also in the language in which it has been framed, Latin. There was some hope that it would be issued officially also in some modern languages like French and English, which are more easily understood by Eastern Catholics as a whole. Instead, the code has appeared in the 'official' language of the church only. Even as it entered into force on 1 October 1991, no unofficial translation was ready, which left most Easterners in the dark as to what law they were bound by since then.

Some feel that the number of times that even a patriarchal church has to refer matters to Rome or get the papal assent is too high to be compatible with the autonomy that is its prerogative. For example, the patriarch may not transfer the patriarchal see even with the unanimous vote of the episcopal synod – it is not enough to inform the pope before or after, but his prior consent is needed (c. 57 § 3). On the other hand the pope can suppress a patriarchal church (sic) even without consulting anyone (c. 57 § 1).

Conclusion

No doubt, compared to the former legislation, the new code CCEO grants to the Eastern Catholic churches greater autonomy. This would be called decentralization in the West. From an oriental standpoint it is the recovery of the ancient synodal structure of church government, which was absorbed in the West by the extension of the Roman primacy. This recovery, paradoxically enough, is due to the concern for tradition among the oriental churches and not so much to any modern democratic ferment.

'Thanks to their traditional structure within the one Church of Christ, the Oriental Churches have, to a certain extent, adhered to the principle of subsidiarity all through the ages, even if without explicit reference to it.'[27] So ran a statement in the guidelines for the codification. And it added: 'The new code should limit itself to the codification of the discipline common to the Oriental Churches, leaving to the competent authorities of these Churches the power to regulate by particular law all other matters not reserved to the Holy See.' This principle of subsidiarity has been applied to a great extent at the patriarchal level, but not much at the eparchial or parochial levels, and only somewhat at the primatial level. In CCEO little power is shared with the laity, and the deaconess has dropped out. From a democratic standpoint, CCEO is as clerical and as male as CIC, traits on which the future may have a different judgment to make from that of the present code, if the church lets itself be further humanized and socialized or draws more on the early Christian tradition.

Notes

1. *Codes Canonum Ecclesiarum Orientalium*, in *Acta Apostolicae Sedis* 82, 1990, 1033–363. Promulgated on 18 October 1990, it entered into force on 1 October 1991.

2. *Synodus* and *concilium* are synonymous in usage. See W. Aymans, *Das Synodale Elemente in der Kirchenverfassung*, Munich 1970, 8.

3. P. Duprey, 'La structure synodale de l'Eglise dans la théologie orientale', *Proche Orient Chrétien* 20, 1970, 123–45.

4. Already in the second century synods were held on issues like Montanism and the date of Easter. See C. Hefele–H. Leclercq, *Histoire des Conciles* I, Paris 1907, 127–51.

5. D. Salachas, 'Il principio della struttura sinodale delle Chiese orientali nella legislazione canonica antica', *Nicolaus* 6, 1978, 221–49.

The synodal principle was also applied in churches outside the Roman Empire. In the East Syrian Church the Synod of Joseph in 554, for example, stated: 'The patriarch must do all that he does with the advice of the community. Whatever he arranged will have all the more authority the more it is submitted for the examination of more numerous bishops' (c. 7); this canon further enacted, like CCEO, a double synodal structure which is astonishingly modern (J. B. Chabot, *Synodicon Orientale*, Paris 1902, 358–9).

6. Unlike 'democracy', the term 'monarchy' has a Christian theological tradition. I use it here in the juridical sense of government with all powers cumulated in one person.

7. G. Nedungatt, 'Ecclesia universalis, particularis, singularis', *Nuntia* 2, 1976, 75–87; J. D. Faris, *The Communion of Churches: Terminology and Ecclesiology*, New York 1985.

For a dogmatic appreciation of the Eastern triadic church structure, see G. Greshake, 'Die Stellung des Protos in der Sicht der römisch-katholischen dogmatischen Theologie', *Kanon* IX, 1989: 'The "Protos" and His Jurisdiction', 17–50.

8. On church *sui iuris*, see I. Zuzek, 'The *Ecclesiae sui iuris* in the Revision of Canon Law', in R. Latourelle (ed.), *Vatican II. Assessment and Perspectives*, Vol. II, New York 1989, 288–304. Like the author, I, too, keep the Latin term *sui iuris*, which is difficult to translate. The literal meaning 'autonomous' can be misleading in certain contexts.

9. This fourth group of churches is not given any specific name but is called simply 'Other Churches *sui iuris*'. The word 'other' refers to a fourth category exclusive of the foregoing three. So I render it 'remainder churches'.

10. A hierarch is a church official invested with sacred power (*hierarchia*), ranking with a bishop or higher (CCEO c. 984), and mostly equivalent to *ordinarius* (CIC c. 134).

11. *Nuntia* 22, 4–5; 28, 34–35. Critics who bemoan the transfer of some powers

from the patriarchs to the synods (*Concilium* 230, 1990, 105–14) abstract from the more ancient tradition (with its ideal norm in canon 34 of the Apostles) and from a truly collegial division of power between the patriarch and the bishops for our times (as evidenced in *Nuntia* 22, 6).

12. *Nuntia* 22, 6.

13. CCEO c. 110. *Synodus Episcoporum Ecclesiae Patriarchalis* is the full Latin title, so worded to avoid confusion with the post-conciliar Roman *Synodus Episcoporum*. Among the Orthodox Churches, the former is usually called holy synod. I shall render the CCEO term as episcopal synod for short, distinguishing it from the Roman synod of bishops.

14. *Nuntia* 5, 10–12.

15. *Pastor Bonus*, nn. 121–5.

16. There are arguments for and against the new Code's general restriction of the jurisdiction of the patriarchs within the territorial borders of the patriarchal church. There are, however, thirteen instances in which the Code extends the powers of the patriarch beyond to the diaspora (*Nuntia* 29, 29–30).

17. The *Synodus permanens* (Latin) = *synodus endémousa* (Greek), dating from the fourth century, had limited legislative, administrative and judicial powers (J. Hajjar, *Le synode permanent, Or Chr Analecta* 164, Rome 1962). The members live in the patriarchal curia or nearby for easy and frequent convocation.

18. CCEO does not regard the Orthodox model as an ideal. Moreover, the pattern varies in the Orthodox Churches. See S. N. Trojanos, 'Die Synode der Hierarchie als höchstes Verwaltungsorgan der einzelnen Autokephalen Orthodoxen Kirchen', *Kanon* II, 1974, 192–216.

19. P. Huillier, 'Le concile oecuménique comme autorité supreme dans l'Eglise', *Kanon* II, 1974, 128–42.

20. The 34th canon of the Apostles (apocryphal, but from the second/third century, though the collection of the Canons of the Apostles is from the late fourth century) does not ground but surpasses both the Orthodox view of the primacy of honour in terms of *primus inter pares* (first among equals) and the Catholic doctrine of the primacy of jurisdiction. Cf. *Kanon* v, 1981: *The Church and the Churches. Autonomy and Autocephaly*, 92–9; 140–3.

21. See *Kanon* III, 1977: *The Position of the Laity in the Law of the Oriental Churches*. In the Russian Church four laymen have been members of the patriarchal synod and in charge of financial and other such administrative matters (p. 37). The laity have a part in the election of the patriarch in the Coptic Church (p. 49), in the Serbian Church (p. 144) and in the Bulgarian Church (p. 152). In this last, lay people share in the legislative power of the clerico-lay assembly as well.

22. *Yogam* is roughly an indigenous institution combining the pastoral council and the eparchial convocation, but both at the eparchial and at the parish levels the laity share in decision-making not only in the administration of temporal goods but in the selection of the clergy, in enjoining penal sanctions for violations of discipline, etc. (*Nuntia* III, pp. 160–161).

23. *Nuntia* 3, 1976, 58, 60; 7, 1978, 20; 11, 1980, 85–6.

24. According to Vatican II, a distinction is to be made: 'The deposit of faith or truths is one thing, the manner of expressing them is quite another' (GS 62). This principle is applied in a critical examination of the supreme church *magisterium* in G. Nedungatt, 'The Teaching Function of the Church in Oriental Canon Law, *Studia Canonica* 23, 1989, 39–60; see 48–51.

25. *Nuntia*, 28, 1989, 29–31; 29, 1989, 54–8. A motion signed by eight members in the plenary assembly expressed dissatisfaction with the canons of title III and called for their reworking. But, after some discussion, under pressure of time, the assembly opted to pass on to the pope an avowedly unsatisfactory alternative draft to do with it what he thought best. And title III remained unchanged.

26. W. De Vries, *Orient et Occident. Les Structures Ecclésiales vues dans l'Histoire des Sept Premiers Conciles Oecuméniques*, Paris 1974: 'For the East, the structure of authority is conciliar' (Y. Congar, Presentation, ibid., 3–4).

27. *Nuntia* 3, 'Guidelines for the Revision of the Code of Oriental Canon Law' (p. 21).

(b) Postconciliar Structures

Experiences of National Synods in Europe After the Council

Bernard Franck

Framework and limits

The geographical framework is that of Western-Central, largely German-speaking, Europe: the two Germanies (the Federal Republic and the Democratic Republic),[1] Austria, the Helvetic Confederation or Switzerland, Luxembourg and the Netherlands. The chronological framework is the decade which followed the end of the Second Vatican Council (1962–1965), i.e. between 1966-67 and 1975–76: all the experiences took place in this period. Finally, these are 'national' experiences, i.e. synods which are not diocesan but which relate to a group of ecclesiastical areas coinciding with the national frontiers of the countries under consideration.

I. Vatican II: the starting point for synodical renewal

Following the *aggiornamento* advocated by Vatican II, the synodical principle experienced a 'new topicality'[2] in the Latin church. This reassertion of the synodical principle in the life and structures of the church was desired at all levels: parochial, diocesan, regional and national. The encouragement lavished by the Council on the 'episcopal conferences' (already constituted or to be constituted), on the various 'diocesan councils' (to be set up) and even on the 'parochial council' (to be set up) is manifest proof that in its overall reflection on the People of God Vatican II wanted to restore the collegiality of the episcopal body, the autonomy of the particular churches in the communion of the universal church, the active place of the laity in this church and these churches, a mode of being and sharing, of communicating and exchanging, of giving and receiving which is characteristic of synodicality and the distinctive feature of the common life of Christians.

So it is not surprising that in the wake of Vatican II a number of national episcopates wanted to seize the opportunity of setting up and developing structures of a synodical type within their countries.

Among these initiatives, alongside the diocesan synods proper it is worth drawing attention to a quite original type of synodical assembly, the framework of which was a country. Such assemblies functioned in accordance with a particular statute and modes of procedure *praeter legem*. They truly provided 'unique' experiences in the sense that we do not find similar experiences before them nor shall we find such experiences after them.

II. Experiences of national synods in the Germanophone areas

1. The Pastoral Council of the Netherlands

What is wrongly called 'the Dutch Council'[3] developed in three main phases: first from January 1968 to April 1970; then from 1970 to 1972 under the title 'Pastoral Council'; and finally, from 1977 to 1979, under the appellation 'National Pastoral Consultation'. To begin with it was generally called the '*National* Pastoral Council' because in fact the (Catholic) ecclesiastical province of the Netherlands coincided with its national limits. However, this was neither a 'plenary' (= national) nor a 'provincial' council in the strict technical sense of the term, since it was not convened or composed, nor did it act in accordance with the canonical regulations then in force governing one or other type of 'council' (plenary or provincial).

To avoid any misunderstanding – for the media and the public at large readily spoke of a 'council' and a 'national council' – the Holy See called for the name to be changed, first by the dropping of the technical term for council, and finally to 'National Pastoral *Consultation*'.

Furthermore, as an extension of the 'National Pastoral Council' the Dutch bishops had envisaged the creation of a permanent national advisory council composed of representatives of all the orders of the people of God (bishops, clergy, religious, laity). However, Rome was opposed to this, as it was later to be opposed to a similar demand from the Swiss bishops, for fear that 'the authority of the bishops and their special place in the church might not be sufficiently safeguarded in the statutes of this body' (*Documentation Catholique* 1627, 1973, 242). In fact, according to the draft statutes for this advisory council, this would have had a power of decision, since the majority of its members would have been designated by 'the base' and not by the bishops. So from this moment on the Holy See showed that it was unwilling to give synodical organs – of whatever kind – more than a purely consultative function. We know that because of the tensions which persisted in the Catholic Church of the Netherlands and which took a dramatic turn in 1978/79, Pope John Paul II, newly elected, suspended the consultation indefinitely and convened a 'particular synod' of the bishops of the ecclesiastical province of the Netherlands in Rome.

According to the spirit and the letter of the documents of Vatican II, the dominant concern of the 'Dutch Council' had been to bring together as closely as possible the faithful of all categories and all conditions for the discussion of burning questions, some of which had been touched on by the ecumenical council and some of which had not, to increase awareness of the co-responsibility of all in the major concerns of the church, and also to give an opportunity for equal participation to the representatives of non-Catholic churches, since one of the objectives of Vatican II had been to give a new impulse to the ecumenical movement.

In its composition, its method, its work and the position of the episcopate, the 'Dutch Council' existed and functioned *praeter legem*, i.e. outside the canonical norms in force. At a first stage it was not too concerned with questions of procedure and law; it worked without a precise statute or a well-defined agenda. There was a concern to allow the faith and the imagination of the faithful to be expressed freely, to emerge without constraints of a legal kind. However, it soon becomes clear that law and rules of procedure have their importance particularly in avoiding excesses, channelling confrontations, and putting issues in some order of priority. A para- or perisynodical assembly cannot function correctly without 'rules of the game' which all approve and observe. Furthermore, the similar assemblies which were in preparation here and there (in Germany, in Austria and in Switzerland) were to learn the lesson and pay more attention to questions of 'rules' and 'procedures'.

In spite of all its flaws and blunders, its excesses and its impasses, which led to mistrust and alienation in Rome and elsewhere, the 'Dutch Council' cannot be regarded as a failure or a purely negative experience, which is what some people are tempted to make it. It showed that the co-responsibility of the baptized can come to full fruition when the participation of each of the faithful is encouraged, respected and orientated for the benefit of the whole people of God. A new confidence and reciprocity between bishops, clergy and laity was aroused and developed; mutual responsibility was cultivated and promoted; and a common interest in the great needs of the world and the church was heightened and refined. Now these are the characteristic features of the 'togetherness of Christians'.

2. The Common Synod of the German dioceses[4]

Several details should be noted. The initiative for the synod came from below, from the base. It was on the occasion of the Essen Katholikentag in September 1968 that the 'Critical Catholicism' group called for a national council to be held on the model of the 'Dutch council'. Now according to the canon law then in force a council or synod could only be convened by the pope or the bishop. This proposal from the grass roots was welcomed by the conference of bishops, which set up a working party for the preparation of the 'Common Synod of the Dioceses of the Federal German Republic'. This was the second special feature. In fact, the holding of a synod common to all the dioceses of the same country was also a novelty, since canon law did not provide for any 'common synod'. The German bishops submitted their project to the Holy See, which approved it. This was a third special feature, for the 'common synod' was not presided over by a legate nominated directly by the Holy See – as would have had to be the case with a 'national synod' – but by the president of the German conference of bishops.

From the preparatory phase of the synod onwards, two things could be noted: First, the canonical dispositions which then governed the convening, composition and theme of a 'national synod' (called a 'plenary council' by the 1917 Code) were no longer suited to the pastoral and ecclesiological situation created by Vatican II. So new formulae had to be found. Secondly, while the meaning and content of the synodical principle was being renewed, there was a concern not to abandon the 'hierarchical principle' in the sense that the bishops did not have control over the synod and only exercised their right as a last word (equivalent to the right of veto). So we can see how in taking up the synodical movement, the theory behind which came from Vatican II and which had been put into practice by the Dutch National Council, the German bishops were able to channel and guide it, avoiding mistakes.

The 'common synod' stood out by its composition alone: 164

ecclesiastics (including the 58 bishops) and 153 lay people (including two religious brothers and ten religious sisters).[5] It will be noted that the total number of laity did not exceed that of the clergy. This was one of the essential and constant conditions laid down by the Holy See for the holding of the common synod, as for all the other similar synodical assemblies. All the members of the synod enjoyed the right of a deliberative vote, which indicated the perfect equality of all involved, whether bishops, priests, religious or lay. Furthermore, the members of the synod, even the members chosen at the level of parishes, movements or associations, were not mandated by those who elected them. They had complete freedom of discernment and decision.

The extent of the decision-making power of the plenary assembly was full in all the spheres in which the presidency, in accord with the conference of bishops, gave it this competence. However, resolutions could not be passed on issues on which the conference of bishops decreed that for reasons of faith or morality (relating to the universal church) it could not give its approval. These resolutions included wishes as well as recommendations and prescriptions. When the bishops felt that resolutions could not be promulgated in the dioceses, they had to be commuted to recommendations or wishes.

As we have just seen, although it was an organ with constitutional rights to participate in decision-making, the common synod remained dependent on the bishops. Still, while affirming their prerogatives – by the possibility of using their veto – the bishops at any rate encouraged the active participation of all members of the synod in the *munus regendi*. And once resolutions had been adopted by the synod as such, they can be seen as the human expression of the 'symphony' characteristic of ecclesial communion.

It follows from these observations that the common synod occupied an intermediate position between a 'purely consultative' organ and a 'fully deliberative' organ, i.e. one that is completely master of its decisions. It had a constitutional right of participation in a special genre. Like all decision-making organs, it was able to vote resolutions with the force of law, but by reason of the various dependent relationships in which it stood (to the bishops and the Holy See), it remained a hybrid organ. However – and here the common synod differed from those of the Democratic German Republic, Austria, Switzerland and the Netherlands – it had the power of decision as a last resort and as an obligation in matters on which neither Rome nor the conference had imposed or would impose their veto.

We should also note that the synod addressed a certain number of 'wishes' (*vota*) either to the conference of bishops or to the Holy See.

Among those transmitted to Rome we might note: permission to use new eucharistic prayers, provisions for women to become 'readers' or 'acolytes', a reformation of canon law in the direction of the effective equality of women and men, a study of the possibility of admitting women to the diaconate, a re-examination of the rules for the laicization of married priests, giving them the possibility of exercising diaconal functions, authorization for the bishops of the Federal Republic to organize a common synod every ten years which would retain the status of that worked out for the 1971–1975 synod, the removal of the obstacles to so-called marriages of mixed religion, the introduction in the future code of new impediments like deceit, immaturity, and a lack of capacity for sharing life and love. The Holy See gave the green light to only a limited number of these wishes.

To sum up: the common synod was an ecclesial assembly made up of bishops, priests and laity. All had an equal voice in decision-making, where a two-thirds majority was always required (a departure from the traditional rule, which required conciliar or synodical decisions to be taken with a virtually unanimous vote). These decisions were valid only for the Federal Republic. They could have an obligatory character for the whole territory of this republic if the conference of bishops had given its consent in advance.

3. The Pastoral Synod of the Democratic Republic

'The Pastoral Synod of the Jurisdictional Constituencies of the Democratic Republic of Germany' (its official name) deserves a separate place among the experiences of national synods presented here.

In fact the seven constituencies which met in the Berlin Conference of Ordinaries included only one true diocese (Meissen); the other six were parts of dioceses situated in the Federal Republic which had been cut in two following the Second World War. So here there was a real 'national' synod, in the sense that the national frontiers of the Democratic Republic of the time were determinative and not the limits of the dioceses, as was the case for all the other similar synods. (The one exception was Switzerland, where the synod included the principality of Liechtenstein, which is a dependency of the diocese of Chur, situated in the Helvetic Confederation.)

Because of the particular political situation in which the Catholics of this country found themselves, the synod tried constantly to preserve and emphasize its purely pastoral and ecclesial character, without 'political' interference or aims. From beginning to end the bishops kept a firm hand on the synodical assembly at the sessions in which they participated, taking part in the discussions but not in the votes. They, too, had made sure that the total number of lay members of the synod did not exceed the bar of 50%. Similarly, they vetoed the possible establishment of a 'permanent pastoral counsel' in which the laity would have had a majority. This mistrust of the lay element was fully justified in the political context of the time. Put on guard by the unfortunate experiences of the Orthodox and Protestant churches under the Communist regime, which by reason of their synodical structures often comprised a marked percentage of laity at every level of responsibility in the church (parishes, deaneries, dioceses) and a good part of whom were paid by the current regime, the bishops of the Berlin Conference of Ordinaries systematically barred laity from holding posts of responsibility in the Catholic Church. Now that Communism has collapsed in the Democratic Republic we can see how well founded this prudence was, after the discovery of the perverse policy of the authorities of the old regime which consisted in spying on and infiltrating all organizations – including those of the churches – to make them 'corridors' for transmitting the official ideology.

Thus the Berlin Conference of Ordinaries fixed the beginning and the end of the synod; its president (the Bishop of Berlin) presided over it, and the Conference of Ordinaries made the agenda. Furthermore – by virtue of the statute adopted by the Berlin conference and approved by the Holy See – the resolutions of the synod were only pastoral recommendations addressed to the conference of bishops, which remained in charge of deciding whether or not it should give them force of law by an explicit act of promulgation.

However, this mode of procedure on the part of the bishops of the Democratic Republic, firm and resolute, should not lead us to forget that the synod had been prepared for by a vast consultation of all the Catholic population (no less than 150,000 replies came into the committee responsible for establishing the main themes of discussion on the basis of reactions coming in from the base) and that interest in the synod was sustained at all levels of this community. Finally, it should be noted that the synod adopted nine documents, of which *Glaube heute* ('Belief Today'), which sums up all the others, can bear comparison with the basic text of the common synod of the Federal Republic, *Unsere Hoffnung. Ein Bekenntnis zum Glauben in dieser Zeit* ('Our Hope. A Confession of Faith for Our Times').

4. The Austrian Synodical Process[6]

After the end of Vatican II a number of Catholic figures in Austria called for the convening of a 'national council', the aim of which would be to apply the decisions of the ecumenical council, adapting them to the particular situation of the country. This 'national council' never took place as such.

By contrast, for several years afterwards, synods were to be held in most of the Austrian dioceses. They had differing fortunes. However, awareness soon arose of the need to co-ordinate the work of the diocesan synods at a national level. Put on their guard by the experiences of the 'Dutch Council', and wanting to avoid clashes with Rome, the bishops abandoned ideas of a 'common synod' of the dioceses of their countries, but in 1972 adopted an 'Austrian synodical process' which differed from both the Dutch and the German approaches. While taking their inspiration for the redaction of its statute and its procedure from the German Common Synod, they added some further safeguards so that no problems could arise. Besides, Rome could not have had any objections, since this was not a real 'common synod', far less a 'national council', but a simple 'pastoral consultation' at the national level. However, subsequently the process came to be called the 'Austrian Synod', and the bishops did not reject this label. The ÖSV – the German acronym for the process – held three sessions, two in 1973 and one in 1974. The bishops played an active part in the discussions and participated in the voting on equal terms with other members of the synod. Cardinal König, then archbishop of Vienna, had stated that the bishops wanted to work as a team with the delegates; that they considered the delegates partners and not people who simply carried out episcopal decisions. At the same time he recalled that the conference of bishops could not be the executive organ of the synod. The Austrian synodical process progressively succeeded in interesting a large number of those who had been sceptical and indifferent – often for opposite reasons – and in setting up at national level a kind of consultative church as a result of the seven diocesan synods which had been held in parallel beforehand.

Among the positive results, we should note the adoption, by a large majority, of four documents. Concrete measures were taken towards the creation of a permanent structure of national consultation and coordination. This would guarantee the implementation of the decisions of the synod, and the preservation, indeed the reinforcement, of a synodical spirit. Similarly, the positions that the Catholic Church of Austria had to take no longer appeared as ukases or Diktats pronounced by the bishops from on high, isolated and disconnected from the rest of the faithful, but as the result of a process of semi-permanent consultation and dialogue in which all the people of God had taken part and had been able to have its say, without denying the bishops their own responsibility, which is to say the last word.

Today, almost twenty years on, we must recognize that the majority of these good resolutions have in practice remained a dead letter, and that the relative enthusiasm which marked the decade between 1965 and 1975 has given place to the moroseness and bitterness, the resignation and the increasingly massive defection, of numerous Catholics, particularly because of a whole series of matters – in particular the nomination by Rome of bishops thought to be integralist and retrograde – which have marked the life of Austrian Catholics over these last years.

5. The Swiss Synod[7]

What has been called the 'Swiss Synod' or 'Synod 72' (because it began in 1972) was in fact a synchronization of the six diocesan synods with inter-diocesan assemblies. This original formula differs as much from the German formula as from the Austrian.

The 'Swiss model' begins from the principle, adopted by the conference of bishops, that the diocesan synods should be prepared together and not separately (as was the case in Austria). From the preparatory phase on, the need was felt to hold sessions common to all the dioceses. In this way the holding of diocesan synods and the meeting of inter-synodical assemblies were combined and synchronized. This original procedure had the advantage of neither offending the Holy See nor getting up the backs of the Swiss Catholics, who differ widely (three races, four languages and as many cultural spheres) and are strongly attached to their local (cantonal) characteristics. Truth to say, in the eyes of both the members of the synod and the public at large, the diocesan synods were the most important. No matter: the very fact that the authorities and the lay faithful from all the regions were getting together – and for many people this was the first time! – made it possible to emerge from a degree of provincialism and to have useful exchanges about specific experiences. In fact in Switzerland an attempt was made to begin not from the texts of Vatican II but from the experience of the base. Now this experience varied significantly, depending on whether people were in the French-speaking, German-speaking or Italian part of the Confederation. Furthermore, the importance of structures was felt differently: the German-speaking populations attached more importance to them than did the French- or Italian-speakers, for whom active involvement was what counted most. For this reason the question of ecclesiastical structures occupied only a secondary place in the interdiocesan assemblies.

If we take into account the 350,000 replies to the 1,350,000 questionnaires distributed within the framework of the national consultation in preparation for the synod, the exemplary work of the 900 delegates chosen to sit in the diocesan synods, the inclusion of the media in the process of informing and training the wider public, we can claim that the new and unique experience of 'Synod 72' was throughout positive for the Catholic church in Switzerland. All the participants became convinced that constant communication, unceasing dialogue, close collaboration, and a sharing of the main problems aimed at a common solution would from then on prove indispensable.

If the literary and theological quality of the documents adopted – twelve in all – are not up to that of the texts of the Common Synod of the Federal Republic of Germany, we should nevertheless note the structural flexibility and the great manageability of Synod 72. Moreover, the boldness of the proposals made by members of the synods and the courage of the bishops in intervening with Rome can only come as a pleasant surprise from the representatives of a country which has a reputation for being conservative.

The Swiss synod had adopted a resolution aimed at the creation of a permanent office for consultation and dialogue, a kind of embryo 'National Pastoral Council'. This project had been adopted by the conference of bishops, which submitted it for the approval of the Holy See. The Holy See asked the bishops to look for another nomenclature (cf. *Documentation Catholique* 1977: 1729, p. 949 and 1732, p. 505). The one agreed on was 'Interdiocesan Pastoral Forum'. Various sessions of this 'forum' took place from 1978 on: they were an extension of Synod 72 (*Documentation Catholique* 1749, 1978, 847f. and 1756, 1979, 98).

Seen retrospectively, at a distance of more than twenty years, one cannot deny that Synod 72 got a whole church on the march, even if this movement has slowed down and various unfortunate decisions coming from Rome (ecumenism, the nomination of bishops) have discouraged a large number of faithful from continuing their involvement in the church.

6. The Luxembourg Synod[8]

We can pay some attention to the Luxembourg synod. This was in fact a diocesan synod, but since the frontiers of the diocese coincide with those of the state and the customary language of this country is German (or a dialect of German), it is natural to mention this synod in the present study devoted to the national synods of the Germanophone area of Western Central Europe.

Since the creation of the diocese of Luxembourg in 1870, only three synods had taken place there, in 1880, 1922 and 1951. The pastoral and communal perspective which had emerged from Vatican II had been completely absent from these synods.

Active preparation for the synod began in 1970 and continued for two years. Almost 225,000 questionnaires were sent out to all the families (at the time the Grand Duchy comprised only around 350,000 inhabitants). There were more than 80,000 replies (almost 30%). Processing these replies revealed the same essential preoccupations as those of neighbouring countries: deepening and proclaiming the faith; the social and political commitment of Catholics; the liturgy and the sacraments; major questions relating to marriage and the family; justice and peace; foreigners and immigrants (about a quarter of the total population of the country!). The statute signed by the bishop in 1971 and approved by Rome shortly afterwards planned, among other things, the composition of the synod: of 191 members, 96 were clergy or religious, 95 lay. It should be noted that the statute provided for the obligatory participation of at least one third women (religious and lay) – a special feature and 'novelty' worth mentioning.

The synod was spread over twenty sessions: from May 1972 to June 1981, which was another special feature . . . and an absolute record in this kind of exercise. No less than thirteen texts were discussed and adopted by the assembly, in which each member enjoyed the right to vote (but only the promulgation by the bishop of each of these documents gave them the binding force of law in the diocese).

Because of the deep preparation and the exceptional duration of the Luxembourg synod, which allowed a real development of the awareness of the co-responsibility of all the baptized, it can be claimed that this synod had much longer-lasting effects than the majority of those like it, even if over the years the initial enthusiasm has progressively lapsed, to give place to the general moroseness characteristic of the Western countries and the discouragement of a great many laity, who, here as elsewhere, watch helplessly as the church is again taken over by clergy who, as always, are jealous of their prerogatives and find it difficult to share responsibilities.

III. A summary of the gains from synodical experiences

For the first time in the recent history of the Catholic Church, 'national' synods have been able to take place, and with the blessing of the Holy See. However, the experience over this period has been limited in time (between 1965 and 1980) and space (the German-speaking area of Europe). For these experiences have not been taken up and repeated since or elsewhere (at least to my knowledge). The 1983 Latin Code of Canon Law which regulates the holding of councils and synods does not provide any procedure for functioning of the type described above. And it is clear that Rome will be careful about again conceding the same *praeter legem* faculties that it had accorded to the synods described here.

For the first time, too, these synods were not the exclusive affair of the 'clergy', but involved all the people of God, including women. This gain has happily been maintained in the dispositions of the new Code on the composition of councils (plenary) and synods (diocesan). Also for the first time there was a kind of general mobilization of the Catholic population which was everywhere invited to prepare seriously for the work of the synods by deep reflection, discussions in small groups at the base, and continual prayer. One could say that during the decade we have considered, 'the synod' of each of the countries mentioned was the prime concern of the majority of Catholic, and indeed non-Catholic, Christians. There was a deep interest, sometimes a real enthusiasm, for everything that happened at the synods, of which the media made abundant mention.

Each of the six synods described above followed a distinctive course and had a different outcome, despite the numerous similarities which allow us to affirm that in their general configuration and in the results they obtained they were all quite similar.

The bishops always succeeded in affirming and preserving their 'control of operations': in any case this was one of the conditions demanded by Rome for giving the 'green light' to the holding of synods. The number of clergy was always greater than – or at least equal to – that of the laity. The decisions voted on by the synods always succeeded in obtaining the approval of the bishops (in particular) or of the episcopal conferences (in general) so that they became binding norms. And the bishops always observed the synodical 'rules of the game' in granting all the synods equal freedom of speech, favouring wide-ranging debates and encouraging each member to become aware of his or her responsibility, thus facilitating the implementation of the decisions taken when these lay within the field of their competence. They always undertook with courage and promptness to convey to the Holy See the recommendations or wishes of the synod which Rome had to examine and possibly approve (this happened only rarely). Finally, the synods were aware and could experience how the way in which they discussed and decided on matters in the church differed markedly from the procedures common in a so-called democratic society. It became more evident to them that the 'power' in and of the church could not be compared with that of the political world, that the 'sovereignty of the people' had nothing to do with the sole sovereignty of the Lord over his people, and that the fact of being the delegates of their brothers and sisters could not be confused with the role of those elected by people as deputies or other members of the representative assemblies of modern democracies.

Even if the technical and legal procedures adopted for the composition of the various groups (praesidium, secretariat, commissions, plenary assembly), for the discussions and debates, for the scrutinies and votes were largely inspired by those practised in the different democratic systems – which the church has always used (cf. the Acts of the Apostles and the councils or synods of the first centuries) – they must not be confused with the democratic form of government practised by Western societies for the last two centuries.

The broad interval of the experiences of national synods after Vatican II has borne abundant fruit and benefited the Catholic Church not only on the theoretical and doctrinal front but also on the practical and experimental front. Bishops and priests have become accustomed to discussing and debating with ordinary men and women, exchanging and sharing with them, thus becoming more aware, together, of their common responsibility in the church for the service of the world and the men and women of our time. Both have learned and relearned that what concerns everyone should be examined and approved by everyone, according to the most authentic ecclesial and canonical tradition.[9]

At a doctrinal level, we can note with satisfaction the positive echoes of the synodical experience to be found in the promotion and setting up, notably in the new Code, of structures of a synodical type, all of which aim at making possible the participation of the largest possible number of faithful in the affairs of the church. Even if for most of the time these structures have only a consultative function, they nevertheless remain indispensable to the welfare of the church, where 'consultation', with certain periods when it has been eclipsed, has always occupied a select place alongside deliberation and implementation, with which it forms a harmonious and 'symphonic' whole.

IV. Conclusions

The experiences of national synods after the Council allow us to draw some conclusions about the way the Catholic Church governs itself. It must take account of the ecclesiological principles affirmed by Vatican II, principles which find their canonical expression in the synergy or confluence of the twofold structure – hierarchical and synodical – which is constitutive of the church.

1. The ecclesiological principles of Vatican II

There can be no doubt that Vatican II clearly stressed both the common participation of all the faithful (baptized, ordained and 'consecrated') in the triple prophetic, priestly and royal function of Christ (*Lumen Gentium* 10, 31, 34–35) and their true equality and equal dignity in Christ (ibid., 32). The same council equally firmly endorsed 'the distinction which the Lord has made between the sacred ministries and the rest of the People of God', namely that in this people, 'by Christ's will some are established as teachers, dispensers of the mysteries and pastors for the others' (ibid.). However, it suggested that the latter are at the service of the people and not vice versa! The hierarchy exists for the people and not the people for the hierarchy. The church is not primarily the 'hierarchs' and then the 'community of baptized', but is primarily – and uniquely – all the baptized, among whom (neither above nor alongside them!) and in the service of whom there are the ordained, those who by the sacrament of order have been invested with the charge to teach, sanctify and direct, not only exercising this triple 'power' for their brothers and sisters, but sharing responsibility with them.

2. The canonical consequences of ecclesiological principles

It follows from these basic affirmations that the church is organized and structured in accordance with a twofold principle, both hierarchical and synodical.

According to the hierarchical principle, there cannot be any governing authority in the church which would eliminate or neglect those who have been charged by God with the ministry of direction. The 'plenitude of power' with which the members of the hierarchy are invested does not come from below, from the people, but is given from above. The hierarchs do not exercise their power (which is different from political power!) in the name of the people but in the name of Christ. They are not the 'representatives of the people' who can be dismissed or demoted by them; nor are they at the mercy of a majority (which can become a minority, depending on circumstances) which dictates to or imposes its will on 'governments'. For this reason the hierarchy (whether it be pope, bishop or the like) keeps its freedom of discernment over against the synodical organs; it remains sole master of the final decision, which it has to take, after consultation with the representative organs of the synodical principle and having weighed the pros and cons of the opinions this gives.

According to the synodical principle, the affirmation and recognition of a co-responsibility of all in the mission of the church can become concrete in institutions which allow this to be implemented. All those who are baptized are the subjects – and not just the objects – of the common responsibility; it bears this responsibility along with all the rest. This co-responsibility is exercised through a variety of organs: synods, councils (particular councils), colleges, conferences, assemblies, etc. (the label does not matter much!). These organs are not a 'counter-power' to the power of the hierarchy; their aim is to act 'with' the hierarchy and 'for' the people, according to a principle different from but complementary to the hierarchical principle.

Finally, these 'synodical' institutions have to be able to function and have to be taken seriously. They must not be treated as 'marginal' or 'peripheral', with no importance or relevance to the life of the church (whether universal or particular). Hierarchs aware of their prerogatives must not either remove them *a priori* or think that they are negligible. For their part, they must be prepared to play the game of synodicality, without which the church of Christ does not truly enjoy all the riches of its members.

In short, there is a *conspiratio in unum*, a common effort to arrive at unanimous (or quasi-unanimous) decisions after exchanges and discussions. Neither the 'ordained', against or without the 'ordinary baptized', nor the latter without the former, but according to the traditional formula *'una cum'*, the ones with the others, the ones for the others. The *'una cum'* (together with) is characteristic of the functioning and the government of the church. This is directed according to the confluence or the convergence of the twofold principle described: both hierarchical and synodical, the two interdependent, and existing only to co-operate for the well-being of the whole while respecting the specificity and the consistency of each.

To sum up: if the church is that described by Vatican II; if the members of the church are co-responsible, each in his or her place and according to his or her condition, then those primarily responsible (the hierarchs) must have the courage to draw the practical conclusions of the ecclesiological statements of the council. So far, unfortunately, they have not done this with sufficient clarity and relevance. In fact, if not in law, the church still is and remains the affair of the pope, the bishops and the priests, when it is – or should be! – the prime concern of all the baptized.

Translated by John Bowden

Notes

1. These two republics have been reunited, in law and in fact, since 1990.
2. B. Franck, *Actualité nouvelle des synodes*, Paris 1980.
3. P. Smulders, *Le concile pastoral hollandais, voix d'une Eglise locale*, IDOC International 23, 1970; J. Kerkhofs, 'The Dutch Pastoral Council as a Model for a Democratic Church Assembly', *Concilium* 7/3, 1961, 135–42; P. Goddijn, 'Ce qu'est le

"Concile pastoral des Pays-Bas'", *Documentation Catholique* 1534, 1969, 173–6.

4. M. Plate, *Das deutsche Konzil. Die Würzburger Synode: Bericht und Deutung*, Freiburg 1975; A. Ness, *Die erste gemeinsame Synode der Bistümer in der Bundesrepublik Deutschland (1971–1975)*, Paderborn 1978; *Gemeinsame Synode der Bistümer in der Bundesrepublik Deutschland. Offizielle Gesamtausgabe*, Freiburg 1976.

5. In canon law these are not considered 'clergy', but laity.

6. See *Herder Korrespondenz* 1974/1, 'Österreich-Synode im Aufschwung', 37–40, and 1974/7, 'Das Ende der Österreich-Synode', 368–72.

7. See *Herder Korrespondenz* 1973/1, 45–8; 1974/2, 104–7; 1975/4, 193–6; 1976/1, 36–40; also *Documentation Catholique* 1972: 1603, 193; 1605, 292; 1618, 944–50; 1975: 1677, 529–31; 1976: 1696, 397–9.

8. See *Luxemburger Diözesansynode*, Offizieller Text der Beschlüsse, Luxembourg 1984.

9. This principle, *quod omnes uti singulos tangit ab omnibus approbari debet*, has been taken up again by the 1983 code, c. 199.3.

Basic Church Structures – Consolidation or Crisis?

New Church Structures without Official Recognition

Berma Klein Goldewijk

The period after Vatican II has been dominated by many conflicts over the identity and organizational structure of the Catholic Church. A number of new structures which have grown up at the base of the church deviate from current structures which have official legitimation. Above all the contribution of Latin American church basic communities to the development and consolidation of democratic conditions within the church has provoked sharp polemic. This has been intensified by the way in which over the past decade a number of attempts have been made to 'parochialize' existing basic communities, to restrict grass-roots initiatives within an institutional church framework. Opposition to this threatens to cause a growing isolation of basic movements from the institutionalized churches. In the meantime this problem has developed beyond the church in a Latin American context and is also beginning increasingly to affect the universal church. The issue here is the recognition by the church that participatory democratic structures at the base are an important way of expressing changed contents of faith within a comprehensive process of liberation.

The relevance of participatory democratic structures to the base of the church is no longer to be noted only with the help of the ecclesiological themes which Vatican II offered here. The field of tension between the particular church and the universal church, or between plurality and collegiality, was still extremely fruitful for interpreting the rise of church basic communities. However, the structural factors which made possible the rise of basic communities in the 1960s and 1970s were quite different from the conditions under which they now exist. Not only has the church-political and ecclesiological context changed decisively, but there have been many shifts in social and political conditions. All over the world, democratic socialist forms of state have almost completely disappeared. It is a fact that socialist models of society have also lost credibility in a number of countries in the south. In the meantime the basic communities have increasingly come to face questions with which the universal church is also confronted: mutual unity, party-political ties, the internal implementation of participatory democracy and the attuning of them to formal types of democracy, the public outcry against unjust social conditions and the replacement or renewal of parochial structures.

In this connection the great themes of Vatican II can only be used to a limited degree as an interpretative framework for the process of consolidating basic communities. Moreover, many of the current ecclesiological conflicts are specifically concerned with the exegesis of the conciliar documents in the shaping of the church and the defining of a political position in new church base structures. In the midst of the deep impasse of the institutional church it is becoming increasingly clear that today's problems in the basic communities no longer fit into the approved conciliar framework of thought and call for new ecclesiological reflections.

The church's *magisterium* is not the flashpoint for the present-day ecclesiological polemic over the question of the democratization of the church. Rather, the spark is provided by the ecclesial identity of movements at the base of the church, which are taking shape as a new model of the institutional church. It is not easy to analyse the present-day contours of this polemic, its content and its effect, all the more so since the legitimation for identifying the basic communities as churches within liberation theology has recently taken very different directions. Thus some liberation theologians, like Gustavo Gutiérrez, argue that the deepening of the identity of basic communities as a 'new way of being the church' is an unstoppable historical process in church and society; Leonardo Boff even argues that they should replace the existing parochial structures. However, others think that the basic communities are caught up in a deeper structural crisis, from which they will find great difficulty in extricating themselves. The only way out is thought to be an increasing integration of basic communities into parochial structures (as argued for by Felix Pastor and Marcello Azevedo), or their development as a new lay movement, with both a break from and some continuity of the movements of Catholic Action (as argued for by José Comblin).

Within the present discussion about the ecclesial identity of the basic communities, this article attempts to clarify the difference between approaches in which they are seen as a renewal and decentralization of the parochial structure, and views in which they are presented as a concretization of new contents of faith and of a new structuring of the church. The issue here is the sociological dimension of the ecclesial identity of the basic communities. This has been investigated thoroughly by Pedro Ribeiro de Oliveira, the Brazilian sociologist of religion. His view is that when people talk about the way in which basic communities give form to the structure of the church, this is a model of church organization which does not primarily have the parish but rather the basic community as a fundamental religious structure. Against this background, the ultimate question is whether the evangelical practices of church basic communities are the harbingers of a radically new, more democratic, structuring of the institutional church or simply a means of adapting the existing structures of the church by which the 'new' will be integrated into the institutional church and neutralized. This gives the classic ecclesiological question of the relationship between Rome and the churches of the Reformation a new setting, the basic communities, so that it seems to have a surprising contemporary significance.

I. Church basic communities in crisis?

In the second half of the 1980s, basic communities in Latin America underwent a number of changes in their internal composition, their identity, and their sociological and ecclesiological foundations. Sociologically, in Brazil most of the basic communities, above all those in the big cities, consist of a wide range of groupings: Bible groups, groups which work from Black or Indian culture, groups concerned with street children, human rights, liturgy and so on. Each of these groupings is relatively autonomous and has direct connections with other basic communities. Most of these groups are represented, often in rotation, at diocesan level, in the so called 'Areas Pastorais' (pastorates), like the Pastoral Negro, Pastoral Indigena, Pastoral Biblio, etc. These 'Pastorais' are recognized by the church hierarchy as church organizations. Representatives of these diocesan 'Areas Pastorais' meet at a supra-diocesan level in the so-called 'Regionais' (regional assemblies). And since 1975 these have in turn met at a national level in the 'Encontros Intereclesiais', which are held roughly every two years. Within this comprehensive structure there is an intensive exchange and circulation of symbols, insights, projects and analyses.

In this process, which has taken shape above all in Brazil, the diversity of cultural, ethnic, racial, gender-specific and religious identities has been rediscovered as an important part of being the church, and at the same time as the foundation for a combination of political forces. Many people underestimate the importance of this process and suppose that the effect of the politicizing of the basic communities from the beginning of the 1980s is the decisive internal factor in their internal crisis. In this connection some people point to the disappearance of a number of politicized cadres from the basic communities, making them popular organizations which are not bound by the limitations of the church *magisterium* in implementing their political options. Others stress that people leave the church basic communities for other urban religious movements because they think that the basic communities put too much stress on the formation of a critical and political consciousness. The standpoint of the official church side is that Catholicism is too one-sidedly turned into a legitimation of political options.

For their explanation of the crisis of the Latin American basic communities, a variety of sociologists of religion go back to the rise of these communities. They see this as the consequence of a preconceived pastoral plan by the Latin American conference of bishops. In this view, basic communities are a solution to structural problems of identity (a lack of priests and a by-passing of parochial structures) programmed by the bishops, with which the Latin American church has been wrestling since the middle of the 1960s. They think that the strategic option under this plan aimed at salving the institutional stability of the church and increasing its social influence.

However, the much-discussed crisis which characterizes the present course of development in the basic communities comprises a complex interplay of both external and internal factors. Within the short space available here I shall be concerned primarily with (*a*) the ecclesial legitimation of the identity of the basic communities which has been on the wane since the beginning of the 1980s, and (*b*) the new Romanizing of the institutional church which has been carried through simultaneously, now no longer in the framework of Vatican I but in the wake of Vatican II.

II. The waning of official legitimation of ecclesial identity

The fact is that the official ecclesial legitimation of basic communities has entered into a serious crisis. From the side of the church hierarchy the 1970s and 1980s were dominated by a concern that the social and political praxis of the base communities might split the universal church. In the 1990s this concern seems slowly to be fading, in an attempt to find through the basic communities an adequate answer to the expansion of urban religious movements, in this case the Protestant sects.

Explicitly neo-conservative and ecclesiocentric strategies from the Vatican and CELAM (the Latin American conference of bishops) are increasingly restricting the legitimate space which the base communities had previously acquired within the institutional church. One example of this development is the change which has taken place in the Latin American episcopate in the period between Medellín and Santo Domingo. The famous conference of Latin American bishops in Medellín (1968) not only aimed at increasing the say of laity in the church but openly opted for a shift in the focal point of the institutional church: the basic social structure of the church was no longer put primarily in the parish but in the basic community. Medellín did not yet speak of 'church' but of 'Christian basic communities' and regarded them as the 'first and fundamental ecclesial nucleus' which had to take responsibility 'for the riches and the spread of the Christian faith'. Moreover, Medellín defined the Christian base community as 'the primal cell of the church's structure, the focal point of evangelization and now an important factor for human progress and development'.[1] With Medellín's official endorsement of the importance of base communities, the last relics of the model of the 'new Christianity' in Latin America disappeared.

The consequences of this for the institutional church and for society were far-reaching. By taking up the option of supporting the basic communities, Medellín aimed at correcting the negative effects of the hierarchical Tridentine church model which had been introduced into Latin America at the end of the previous century, after Vatican I. The conference of bishops legitimated the new awareness of the evangelical identity of the Latin American church, regarded solidarity with the impoverished sectors of the population as the central dimension of the identity of the church, opted for a church which rediscovers its task in the process of liberation, and envisaged renewing the ecclesiological dimension of the church along these lines.

The Third Conference of Latin American Bishops in Puebla made some corrections to the process of Latin American basic communities to the degree that in the ten years which had elapsed since Medellín these had put too much emphasis on the political dimension. This emerges among other things from the strong emphasis that the bishops now put on the 'ecclesial' character of the basic communities. The ecclesiological reading made by Puebla circles round two key concepts: *participatio* (participation and co-responsibility) and *communio* (community and unity). Puebla endorsed the standpoints of Medellín mentioned earlier, recalled *Evangelii Nuntiandi* (no. 58) and spoke of church basic communities as 'an important ecclesial fact that is specific to us and "is a hope for the church"'.

At the same time Puebla saw the basic communities as a 'focal point of evangelization and motive forces for liberation and development'. These standpoints confirm the official church recognition of the basic communities.

In the period since the beginning of the 1980s, however, the church's *magisterium* has begun to dissociate itself openly from the options of the Latin American episcopate. Internal tensions are sharpening between the members of the Latin American episcopate and the Vatican Congregation for the Doctrine of Faith, among other things because of the instructions *Libertatis Nuntius* and *Libertatis Conscientia*, and with them the silencing of Leonard Boff. These tensions are escalating yet again in the nomination of neo-conservatives to be Latin American bishops.

This conservative tendency is also continuing undiminished above all in connection with the recognition of the ecclesial identity of the basic communities. Thus the recent encyclical *Redemptoris Missio* (no. 51) regards basic communities as 'decentralizations and divisions of the parochial community'. The *Documento de Consulta* for the Fourth General Assembly of the Latin American Episcopate in Santo Domingo confirms this doctrinal line.[3] The preparatory document approaches the basic communities above all as a lay movement within the church, and presses for a better co-ordination of the base communities and a clearer connection with and integration into the structures of the local churches. It opts for a more directed pastoral guidance through which 'imperfections' in interpretation and application of the Bible and the social doctrine of the church to situations of injustice and oppression can be avoided. The option for the poor is directly connected with 'promocíon humana', the furthering of human dignity, in the light of the social teaching of the church (no. 121). Theologically, the document draws the description of the option for the poor above all from *Libertatis Conscientia* (nos. 146 and 311). The centres where new culture is produced (the media, institutions concerned for peace, liberation, ecology, international relations) are transformed into a mission field and a terrain for 'new evangelization' (107). In short, the document encourages a greater unanimity within church structures, with the aim of achieving a more convincing missionary witness outside, above all in the face of the expansion of new religious movements.

In conformity to this perspective, many Latin American bishops are using their ecclesiastical authority to integrate basic communities into the existing structures of the parish, as a result of which they are put under the direct jurisdiction of parish priests. Here the Latin American episcopate, the majority of whom were nominated by John Paul II, has the decisive power of decision in determining whether ecclesial base communities can continue as a relatively autonomous form of being the church to the base in their diocese.

III. Romanization and parochialization

On the basis of this account we can again take up the question in what sense the basic communities offer a foundation for a restructuring of the institution. Here the basic problem relates to the historical possibilities of reorganizing them around the parochial structures laid down by the process of Romanization in Latin America. Officially the parish forms the basis of the local (particular) church, tied to a diocese. However, where basic communities are taking shape as a new model of the church, as 'communio-community' church or a 'church of the poor', this has far-reaching consequences. In that case there is a model of a church whose basic structures do not primarily rest on the Romanized parish but on a network of church basic communities. In this perspective the sacramentality and institutional incorporation into parochial structures imposed by Romanization would be overcome.

One of the most important fields of tension is now the degree to which the basic communities can take over the tasks and structure of the traditional parishes. Here reference is often made to the fact that the basic communities often give better form to the communal dimension of the Christian faith than parishes, since they are less anonymous and offer more space and freedom for circulating ministries and services. Leonardo Boff adopts the standpoint that while the basic communities are not an alternative for the whole of the church, they should gradually become institutionalized, should spread and become universal, as also happened with parochial structures between the twelfth and the fourteenth centuries. In his view the parish as a social basis for the structure of the institutional church will be replaced by the basic community. For others, however, the resolution of the existing tension does not lie in a substitution, but in an increasing integration. This should take shape through a 'renewal' or 'revival' of traditional parochial structures through the basic communities. The argument offered in support of this approach is that the basic communities do not yet offer the legal structure that a parish has, a structure that they regard as a necessary condition for the continuance of the church as an institution. The problem in this approach, however, is that by integration, the renewal of Catholicism which the basic communities are bringing about could be completely incorporated into the institution, without in any way necessarily being coupled with an institutional reorientation of the church.

The question around which everything turns is ultimately what factors are seen as most decisive for interpreting the significance of basic communities for the institutional church. It is important here to note that the institutional church does not have any prior given identity which is or is not made concrete in the basic communities. Already at the beginning of the 1980s the Chilean Pablo Richard indicated the limitations of such an understanding of the identity of the church. He argued that if there were already an identity of the church which was given *a priori*, then this definition was a negative identity, because it could be 'lost'. In contrast to an identity existing in advance, an *a posteriori* identity is a consistent identity; it is not a position that can be proved or defined afresh, but a criterion for a Christian radicality which becomes concrete in history yet can never coincide wholly with a particular model of the church, and has constantly to be discovered anew.

In this perspective, the basic communities' message of liberation and redemption does not come primarily from a reorganization of church structures. Faith is revealed in the base communities as the creator of an original church identity, the institutional significance of which no one can as yet see.

Translated by John Bowden

Notes

1. CELAM, *La Iglesia en la actual transformación de América Latina a la luz del Concilio*, Bogotá 1969, 'Pastoral de Conjunto', nos. 10, 11.
2. CELAM, *Puebla. A evangelização no presente e no futoro da América Latina*, Petropolis 1979, no. 629 and 617–57.
3. CELAM, *Documento de consulta. Nueva evangelización, promoción humana, cultura cristiana*, Bogotá, May 1991, pp. 179–80, nos. 401–2.

The Dumont Report

Gregory Baum

On 22 June 1960, with the election of the Liberal Party, began in the province of Quebec a cultural and social upheaval, named the Quiet Revolution, that shook the foundation of the conservative Catholic society. The upheaval initiated a rapid process of secularization. The people of Quebec strove to create for themselves a new collective identity, a secular one, no longer dependent on their Catholic past. The newly-elected government began to take over the network of ecclesiastical institutions that had served society in the areas of education, health and welfare. This process was accompanied by a drastic drop in church membership. After a period of seven years Catholics constituted a minority in Quebec.[1]

The spirit of Vatican II allowed Catholics to participate in the rapid modernization of their society. They believed that the reduction of ecclesiastical power would lead to a flowering of Catholic life. But the emergence of a new, secular outlook began to worry the Quebec bishops. In 1968, they decided to appoint a research commission, presided over by Fernand Dumont, to examine the crisis of the church, and, on the basis of this research, to formulate recommendations for new, more appropriate pastoral policies.

In its structure the Dumont Commission resembled the study commissions set up by the federal or provincial governments of Canada. The Dumont Commission held hearings in various parts of Quebec and received briefs from church groups and church organizations; it commissioned psycho-sociological research on the attitudes and religious values of the Quebec population; and finally it produced a report, the Dumont Report, that summed up the research and made detailed proposals for new pastoral policies.[2]

In 1971 the Commission published the Report, *L'église du Québec: un héritage, un projet*,[3] accompanied by two other volumes, one offering a new reading of the history of the Quebec Church (1608–1970) and the other making available to the public the psycho-sociological research.[4] In 1972 the Commission published three more volumes, a history of Catholic Action in French Canada, a presentation of the opinions and proposals gathered by the Commission, and a synthesis of the Report for use in discussion groups.[5] The Dumont Commission thus produced altogether six volumes.

Who were the members of the Commission? The chairman, Fernand Dumont, a well-known sociologist, worked with eleven other members, including one bishop, a few priests, and several lay men and women, drawn mainly from the Catholic Action movement. One member was identified with the trade union movement.

Rupture and fidelity

To understand the work of the Dumont Commission it is necessary to look at the methodology it chose to employ. How did the Commission proceed from the empirical investigations to the composition of its report? The Commission was confronted by an enormous diversity of opinions. Extremely conservative Catholics wanted the church to return to the pre-conciliar, uniform style in teaching and liturgy. Many of them even hoped that Quebec would again become a Catholic society. On the opposite end of the spectrum were radical Catholics who wanted the church to become fully egalitarian and this-worldly, abandon the distinction between priesthood and laity and involve itself in a mission defined in purely humanistic terms. Between these two extremes were a multitude of opinions and proposals.

Given this diversity, the Dumont Commission adopted two principles of discernment. First, the Commission accepted the historical judgment that the Quiet Revolution was an irreversable societal process, that Quebec had become a secular, pluralistic society, and that the Catholic Church no longer spoke for the whole of Quebec but only for a sector, the community of the faithful. This judgment allowed the Commission to disregard the submissions made by Catholics who yearned for the return of the old Quebec.[6]

The formulation of the second principle was more difficult. The Commission argued that Quebec society and the Quebec church were both engaged in a quest to redefine their collective identity.[7] Phenomeno-logical reflection on the formation of personal and social identities convinced the Commission that overcoming an identity crisis demanded an original response to the new situation and at the same time the preservation of continuity. Both rupture and fidelity were demanded. This twofold reference to past and future was the principle, this time a theological one, that guided the Commission in its recommendations.[8] It decided to name this principle in the title it gave to its final report, *L'église du Québec: un héritage, un projet*.

The church faithful to the past is capable of responding to new challenges in the present. In the words of the Report, pastoral policies are always 'des stratégies du provisoir'.[9] The church is forever unfinished, a people on pilgrimage, engaged in a series of workshops, 'des chantiers', where they jointly respond to the gospel in the conditions of their day. At the same time, such an ecclesial project is in continuity with the inheritance of the past. In Quebec, the Report explains, this inheritance is the profound solidarity of the church with the people of Quebec through the different phases of its history, first as French colony, then as British colony, and later as Canadian province. This history has allowed the church to assume a strong cultural and organizational presence in Quebec, a position of power that the church defended against those who challenged it by turning increasingly to Rome as source of its own authority and independence. This special historical situation has produced both 'la grandeur' and 'la misère' of the Quebec church.[10] Only now, as Quebec society is assuming greater responsibility for itself, is the church able to define itself anew, this time with greater self-reliance.

What precisely is the heritage to which the church of Quebec must be faithful? The Report singles out three characteristics: (i) the missionary orientation of the Quebec church; (ii) its commitment to French Canadian and later Quebec society; and (iii) its character as a *communio*, as a community of solidarity and shared values. The missionary orientation must now be understood, following *Gaudium et spes*, as the church's readiness to serve 'the world', first the society of Quebec and beyond it, especially the peoples of the Third World. The commitment to Quebec society now demands the humble recognition that Quebec has become a secular, pluralistic society, that the church represents only a minority and that as such it is willing to join the public debate regarding the common good and the future of Quebec society. Because it no longer speaks for the whole, the church is now able to exercise a socio-critical function, a prophetic role, defending the weakest members of society and calling for social and economic justice.

Democratizing the church

Since this article deals with the democratization of the church, it is the third characteristic, the *communio* aspect, the church's communal nature, that is of special importance. To elucidate what fidelity to this heritage means today the Dumont Report introduces three themes, which it calls 'participation', 'pluralism' and 'the toleration of dissent'.[11] Because the church is a communion, the Report argues, it may not be thought of as 'an immutable pyramid throughout the ages nor an inaccessible obelisk'.[12] A highly centralized bureaucracy hides the church's true nature as the communion of the faithful. Communion implies participation. As the Quebec people, mobilized by the Quiet Revolution, have acquired a strong sense of their social responsibility, so have the Catholics among them gained the conviction that they have a collective responsibility for their church as well. 'The democratization of secular life has not failed to influence the expectations of the faithful, whether they be lay people, religious or priests.'[13]

The Report points to the teaching of Vatican Council II on the presence on the Spirit in the people and the ecclesial principle of collegiality to demonstrate that the aspirations of Quebec Catholics are in line with the emerging self-understanding of the church as a whole.

This call for democratization does not question the episcopal-papal structure of the church, which Catholics regard as institutions *iure divino*. The Report claims that 'the introduction of democratic ways can go a long way without compromising the hierarchical structure'.[14] What is demanded is wider consultation and co-operation in decision-making. The faithful and their priests want to participate in some way in the decision-making process that affects the church's pastoral message and policies. To preserve the character of the church as communion it is necessary to create certain 'lieux de participation' in order to give a concrete form to the co-responsibility of the baptized. We shall see below what institutional recommendations were made by the Dumont Report.

Because of the church's heritage as communion, it should now be possible to preserve solidarity among the faithful in the face of the internal pluralism of the Catholic community. Since the renewal of institutions is a gradual process and affects some people more quickly than others, the church as project must affirm a certain internal pluralism. More than that, because the present church has an urgent concern for justice in society, the different political trends adopted by Catholics are bound to produce a certain pluralism within the church, with some preferring moderate strategies and others opting for more radical ones. Finally, there exist within the church differing religious aspirations and differing theological interpretations of the principal thrust of the gospel, all of which deserve respect. This is the third source of pluralism within the church.

The Report recommends that the church as project, faithful to its heritage as *communio*, welcome such pluralism among Catholics. The Report reminds its readers that already Pius XII recognized the need for an informed public opinion in the church[15] and that more recently, Paul VI asked Catholics to avoid 'a single word' and 'a single solution' in response to today's challenges.[16] The Report concludes that 'one must denounce the tendency of long standing, also among lay people, to reduce the response to a complex set of problems to a single official definition, especially coming from Rome'.[17] There is room in the church for responsible dissent and respectful opposition. 'There exists in the Church a Christian ethics of dissent, criteria of Gospel authenticity permitting protest, in fact a pluralism inscribed in the Catholic tradition marked as it is by tensions. It is important to remind those who cling to the "letter" – to their "letter" – of the transcendent claim of the Spirit.'[18]

In recommending participatory procedures in the church and welcoming a certain pluralism, the Report believes to be faithful to its principle of double reference, 'rupture and fidelity'. We recall that the Commission disregarded the radical proposals made by certain Catholic groups because they did not protect the church's historical continuity and hence its spiritual collective identity. The Commission regarded its own recommendations as responsible, moderate, and balanced. The Report argued that the church must democratize its social existence to remain faithful to its spiritual foundation and its evangelical mission.

Democratic structures

An important section of the Report, dealing with the structures of the church, makes a series of institutional recommendations.[19] Here the Report clarifies what it means by 'lieux de participation'. The Report proposes an institutional strategy along two lines: the creation on various levels of clearly defined 'centres of decision-making' which formulate pastoral policies, and correspondingly the creation of 'common assemblies' that invite the participation of the people affected by the policies made by their respective 'centre of decision-making'.[20]

What does this proposal mean for the parish? The Report recommends that in all parishes there be created a 'pastoral council' open to lay men and women and 'an episodic assembly' that at certain intervals convokes all the members of the community to reveal their concerns, evaluate present policies, enlarge the concern of the parish, and initiate new pastoral ventures.[21] Since the 'pastoral council' is to be the decision-making body, the Report suggests that the parish priest not act as a man of authority but rather become a 'facilitator' and 'leader of a team'.

It should be added that the Commission debated at great length whether or not the parish itself was still a useful and viable institution.[22] Parishes in small towns and villages have retained much of their vitality. But in the big cities, especially Montreal, parishes were in trouble. Their difficulty was caused in part by the rapid secularization of the population and in part by the trend among the faithful to form smaller, more intimate and more involving groups and stay away from the parishes to which they belonged. The Commission eventually decided to defend the institution of the parish but recommended that the parish priest welcome the formation of smaller groups and try to be present to them. The Commission recognized that the greatest vitality in a religious organization is usually found in its smaller groups, movements and networks. These formations should be encouraged, the Report argues, even if they should choose to remain independent of the ecclesiastical structures, as long as their spiritual concern is in keeping with the basic orientation of the church as a whole.

The Report also recommended the creation of new institutions, named 'pastoral zones', that would bring together people belonging to different parishes, yet united by common concerns, common conditions or common problems. Such 'zones' could embrace, for instance, the workers of a large neighbourhood, the youth in a certain part of the city, or the unemployed and welfare recipients in an area beyond the limits of a single parish.[23] Here the 'centre of decision-making' would be an appointed 'zone council', possibly made up exclusively of lay people, and the 'common assembly' would be a meeting, held at regular intervals, open to all affected by the zone's activities. The Report expressed the hope that these new institutions would promote a certain de-clericalization of the church's ministry.

The Commission recognized that Vatican II had already suggested the creation of parish councils and in the diocese the setting up of a pastoral council or a council of priests. These institutions were to promote collegiality, dialogue and cooperation in the church. The recommendations of the Dumont Report move in the same direction, but go far beyond the narrow limits set by ecclesiastical tradition to the participation of lay people and to the bishop's power to welcome their participation in decision-making.

Thus the Report proposes the creation in each diocese of a pastoral council, presided over by the bishop, as the 'centre of decision-making', and the convocation at regular intervals of a pastoral assembly that would allow the people and their priests to express their concerns and propose new pastoral orientations.[24] Since the church wants to encourage the various movements in the diocese, representatives of these movements should be made members of the pastoral council. This would bring them into an ongoing dialogue with the bishop and the diocese as a whole and overcome the present condition, where the movements often find themselves misunderstood and exposed to heavy-handed, bureaucratic decisions. If the pastoral council is allowed to assume its full responsibility, then the diocesan bureaucracy, which is presently the locus of many arbitrary and somtimes conflicting decisions, would become an executive organ that implements the decisions made by the pastoral council.

The Report also makes concrete proposals, following the same principle, for interdiocesan structures for the entire Quebec church.[25] The purpose here is to overcome the bureaucratic style of church government, to enhance the co-operation and co-ordination of the church's pastoral projects, and to increase the participation of the laity on all levels of the decision-making process.

The democratization of the church proposed by the Dumont Commission could be implemented within existing Roman Catholicism if the bishops, out of pastoral zeal and love for democratic co-operation, decided to limit the power assigned to them by canon law. Even on the level of the parish, any sharing in decision-making depends on the generosity of the parish priest. But structures that are not written into law but depend on good will of the powerful alone will be fragile and unstable. Implicit in the Dumont Report is the wish that the recommended democratization will one day be approved by the Catholic Church as a whole and inscribed in a new codex of canon law.

Conclusion

The Dumont Report had only a limited impact on the Quebec church. There were reasons for this quite apart from the reticence of many bishops. The secularization of Quebec culture continued throughout the 1970s and 1980s. The enthusiasm of engaged Catholics, produced by the reforms of Vatican II and the rapid transformation of Quebec society, had begun to wane by the time the Report was published in the early 1970s. During its preparation, the interest of Catholics had been intense. The high attendance and the ardent participation at the hearings organized throughout the province had demonstrated to the Commission members widespread, enthusiastic concern for the renewal of the Christian life. This enthusiasm declined in the 1970s.

Still, the Dumont Report was not without influence. The Quebec bishops, supported by a network of social justice groups and centres, adopted a critical, prophetic stance toward the emerging social order. In their pastoral letters they offered a detailed critique of contemporary capitalism and its historical consequences: the widening of the gap between rich and poor, and the marginalization of a growing sector of society. The bishops encouraged vitality, imagination and pluralism within the church. They protected the freedom of theological inquiry and refused to interfere in radical Catholic movements. But the attempt to democratize Catholic institutions has failed.

Notes

1. Gregory Baum, *The Church in Quebec*, Montreal 1991, 15–48.
2. Cf. *The Church in Quebec*, 49–66.
3. *L'Eglise du Quebec: un héritage, un projet*. Montreal 1971.
4. Nive Voisine, André Beaulieu and Jean Hamelin, *Histoire de l'église catholique au Québec, 1608–1970*, Montreal 1971; Norman Wener and Jocelyne Bernier, *Croyants du Canada français I: recherches sur les attitudes et les modes d'appartenance*, Montreal 1971.
5. Gabriel Clément, *Histoire de l'action catholique au Canada français*, Montreal 1972; Norman Wener and Jacques Champagne, *Crovants du Canada français II: Des opinions et des attentes*, Montreal 1972; Yves-M. Cote, *L'église du Québec: un heritage, un projet – Rapport synthese: instrument de travail*, Montreal 1972.
6. *Report*, 43–4.
7. Ibid., 52–9.
8. Ibid., 85.
9. Ibid., 103.
10. Ibid., 64–8.
11. Ibid., 114–28.
12. Ibid., 95.
13. Ibid., 114.
14. Ibid., 115.
15. Ibid., 196.
16. Ibid., 134.
17. Ibid., 135.
18. Ibid., 112.
19. Ibid., 257–89. In an appendix (pp. 295–303) the Report proposes a detailed plan for financing the recommended institutional changes.
20. Ibid., 59.
21. Ibid., 266–7.
22. Ibid., 260–4.
23. Ibid., 268–73.
24. Ibid., 274–80.
25. Ibid., 281–9.

(c)   Other Confessions and Religions

Democracy and Charisma
Reflections on the Democratization
of the Church

Miroslav Volf

I

1. The church is not a 'democracy', but a 'Christocracy'. This was a slogan Karl Barth coined in the 1950s. On one level the slogan is, of course, correct. A 'church' in which the people ruled *as opposed* to God could have nothing to do with the reign of God and could therefore never be a church of God. The church of God is inseparable from the reign of God. Barth's slogan expresses this correctly. At the same time, as it stands the slogan is wrong-headed. It assumes that the debate about democracy in the church is about whether God *or* people should rule in the church. This assumption is, however, fundamentally mistaken, although both the congregational and episcopal traditions have operated (and still do operate) with it.

John Smyth, the first Baptist, rested his whole ecclesiology on the basic theological persuasion that the kingly rule of Christ realizes itself through the *whole* local church. A true visible church is 'Christ's kingdom', the members of it are the 'children of the kingdom' and as such rule in the church. If they need to be subject to anyone for the sake of order, then it is to the government of the *whole* local church. Only then do they stand 'under the government of Christ'. The principle of church government is: Christ rules where the whole local church rules; its polemical point is: Christ cannot rule where the ultimate seat of authority rests with particular people in the church – the bishops.[1] In the episcopal tradition one often encounters the mirror image of this argument. Because Christ comes to a local church through the mediation of a bishop who stands in diachronic and synchronic communion with all other bishops, the bishop is indispensable if Christ is to rule in a local church. Here the principle of church government is: Christ rules where the bishop rules; its polemical point is: Christ cannot rule where the ultimate seat of authority lies in the whole local church.[2]

Both congregational and episcopal traditions insist on the rule of Christ in the church. They accuse each other, however, of subverting this rule by the *way* in which each insists the rule of Christ should be concretely exercised. The main point at issue in the debate between congregational and episcopal traditions about the democratization of the church is therefore not who should rule in the church (people or Christ), but *through whom Christ should exercise his rule in the church* (through the whole congregation or [primarily?] through the bishop).

2. The question whether the rule of Christ in the church requires ecclesiastical 'democracy', 'aristocracy' or 'monarchy' (however one defines these polysemous terms ecclesiologically) is a very complex one. Any theologically responsible answer to it would have to deal carefully with some of the following related issues. First, what is the biblical basis for a particular church government? Does the New Testament clearly favour one or the other form? Do we rather find in it multiple forms of church government suited to various cultures to which the church spread in the first decades of its existence? Second, what in the New Testament ecclesiology (or ecclesiologies) is theologically binding? Are there any God-given structures of the church, or are the structures that we find in the New Testament only more or less adequate forms of inculturating the social reality of the gospel? Third, where is the primary seat of ecclesiality to be found – in the local church or in the universal church? Fourth, what is the nature of ecclesial social reality? Is it simply a particular community of persons or does it also have a subjectivity – a subjectivity that it receives from Christ, since together with him it comprises the 'whole Christ' (Augustine)? Fifth, what is the underlying notion of democracy? To what extent can the modern parliamentary democracy serve as a model? Or is this democracy merely a disguised civil war of interests in which a majority wins by the use of civilized brute force, and as such only a structural expression of prevailing individualism?[3] Does the church as a community

of faith demand its own specific forms of democracy? Sixth, how do the democratic structures and procedures in the church actually function? Is the participation of the people a genuine reality or is 'democracy' simply an ideology that conceals (and thereby perpetuates) the existing authoritarian relations of power?

I cannot address these issues in the confines of this brief article. I will proceed on tacit assumptions about them and concentrate my comments on the relation between democratic structures and spiritual power in the church. Is the participation of the people in decision-making compatible with the rule of the Spirit of Christ? Do democracy and charisma mix? Since the church is the church by the presence and rule of the Spirit of Christ in it, this is one of the most fundamental theological issues that the question of the democratization of the church raises.

II

In an article 'Democratization of the Church?' (the early?) Joseph Ratzinger offered the following brief reflections about the 'charismatic constitution of the church' conceived as a variant of a dominance-free understanding of social relations: 'Historically speaking, charisma is not a democratic but a pneumatic principle, i.e. a term that designates the empowering from above which one cannot control, not a common control from below. The notion of charisma should therefore disappear from the debate about the democratization of the church.'[4] Just as Barth set 'democracy' over against 'Christocracy', so Ratzinger is here, I propose, setting up a false dichotomy between democratic and pneumatic principles. To support my contention, in the present section I will analyse two features of charisms, and then in the following section draw some implications for the nature of ordination and the process of electing ministers.

1. Ratzinger is right when he claims that charisms represent empowering from above; human beings cannot dispose over them as they wish, but the Spirit imparts them 'just as *he* determines' (I Cor. 12.11). But the crucial question in relation to democracy in the church is *how* does the Spirit impart charisms? More precisely, what is the role of the community in the impartation of charisms? Often charisms are thought of as 'sudden' and 'supernatural' phenomena – they come from above, not from below. The only thing people can do is to open themselves for them. (A possible consequence of this view is a dichotomy between offices and charisms: offices are mediated sacramentally through people, charisms are given directly from the Lord.[5]) This model is too simple, however. Paul suggests

that a person should 'eagerly desire' spiritual gifts (I Cor. 12.31; 14.1) and 'excel' in them for the edification of the church (I Cor. 14.12). The 'desiring' of charisms and 'excelling in them' presupposes assessment of one's own inherent or acquired abilities and of the needs of the church. In order to serve others (which is the purpose of charisms) I have to know what others need and what I can offer them. Of course, I cannot simply pick out charisms in accordance with my assessment of myself and of others. Seeking particular charisms makes sense only if I am ready to correct my assessment of myself and of others by their assessment of themselves and of me. For others have to be willing to accept my service. This line of thinking leads us to the *interactional model of the impartation of charisms*. I receive charisms from the Spirit of God through my own interaction with myself – with what I am by birth and with what I have become on the basis of my inborn capacities in a given society – and with the church and the world in which I live. Charisms are the gifts of the sovereign Spirit of God; he does not give them, however, to isolated individuals, but to people in their concrete social and natural settings. So the manner in which charisms are imparted by the Spirit is *essentially communal*.

2. If charisms are given by the sovereign Spirit of God 'just as *he* determines, then one cannot know in advance whether a person is given a charisma in permanent possession or not. This is, I suggest, an implication of the fact that human beings cannot dispose of charisms as they wish. From this it follows that charisms presuppose a permanent process of ecclesial spiritual evaluation. Every charismatic person is received by the church as charismatic in the process of her serving the church. This ecclesial activity of reception has two essential dimensions: a critical one and an ingestive one: 'Test everything. Hold on to the good' (I Thess. 5.21; cf. also I Cor. 14.29; I John 4.1). It would certainly be mistaken to give the primary importance to the critical dimension of reception. Critical evaluation does not take place for its own sake, but serves the authentic reception of the activity of the Spirit. But that does not change the fact that critical evaluation must accompany every charismatic activity in the church. For charisms are always dependent on the concrete activity of the Spirit; that cannot be simply presupposed.

It is important to note that the whole process of reception is not an external addition to charisms, but an essential dimension of them. According to the interactional model, charisms are not given to an isolated individual who is then placed into the church to serve it with her spiritual gifts. Precisely as the gifts of the Spirit, charisms are given in the process of interaction between the charismatic individual and the church. Charisms are always partly conditioned by a concrete church in which a person lives (although they are not *given* by the church). For this reason a church can implicitly or explicitly decide about the presence of charisms in its individual members. To have charisms and to serve with charisms is essentially an *open ecclesial process*.

If this understanding of the relation between charisms and community is persuasive, then empowering from above does not stand in opposition to conditioning from below. Precisely as the gifts of the sovereign Spirit of God, charisms are communally mediated. And if communal mediation is a constitutive feature of charisms, then charisms are not only compatible with ecclesiastical 'democracy'; they seem to presuppose at least some form of implicit 'democracy'. I will try to make this thesis plausible by looking at the nature of ordination and election of ministers.

III

1. I take ministries to be particular forms of charisms. Just like any other service in the church, the ministry of ordained ministers rests, on the one hand, on the calling that is common to all Christians and, on the other hand, on charisms that are peculiar to the ordained ministers. But, since all activity in the church is charismatic, the *ordained* ministry cannot be grounded in charisms as such, but in the specific characteristics of the ministry that the ordained ministers do and in the corresponding peculiar characteristic of charisms they receive. What is specific to charisms of ordained ministry is their relation to the *whole of the local church*.[6] The ordained ministry is grounded in the ecclesial need for the activity in the name of the church in relation to God and the world on the one hand, and in the activity in the name of Christ in relation to the church as a whole on the other.

If ministry is essentially charismatic, then this has important implications for the understanding of ordination (provided that my analysis of the nature of charisms is plausible). First, since charisms are the gifts of the Spirit, the ministerial charisms cannot rest on delegation on the part of the people (as is often claimed in the congregational tradition). For such delegation can mean nothing else than that the ministers have been given their task and authority to perform it by the people and not by the Spirit of God. Second, ordination must take place *through* the people. As I already indicated, ecclesial reception of charisms is an important dimension of their impartation by the Spirit. The same is true also of ministerial charisms. Ordination must be understood therefore as *communal recognition* of a charisma that is given by God. It is a public and festive ending to a much longer ecclesial activity of reception which is part and parcel of the constitution of a ministerial charisma.

2. It follows that the procedures through which a person is ordained must include the participation of the whole local church. First, people must participate in the *act of ordaining*. Since the activity of ministers relates to the whole local church, ministerial charisms need to be recognized by the *whole* church. Ordination is *an act of the whole local church that is led by the Holy Spirit* and not simply of a particular group in the church that perpetuates itself through the institution of ordination (see Acts 6.1–6; 13.1–3). A local church can (and in most cases will) ordain through its representatives – ministers that act in its name (see I Tim. 4.13–14), but the local church must be present at the ordination because the whole local church is the human subject of ordination. The divine calling and gifting of a minister is recognized through the ordaining activity of the whole church. John Smyth rightly claimed, 'They are sent by God to preach whom the church sendeth.'[7]

Second, the whole local church must participate in the *election* of the persons to be ordained. The liturgical act of ordination, whose human subject is the whole local church, is inseparable from the election of the person to be ordained.[8] This is especially the case if the ordination is interpreted as recognition of a charisma (recognition that is, however, not merely extrinsic to the charisma itself). The separation between the two would empty the liturgical consecration of all content and reduce it to spiritual 'rubber stamping'. Just as ordination represents a formal ending of a much longer process of ecclesial reception of ministerial charisms, so also election begins already with the ecclesial reception. Through ecclesial reception of ministerial charisms 'candidates' are either 'chosen' or 'rejected'. Electoral procedures (such as voting) make sense theologically only as a formalized ending of this process of reception.

IV

In a recent book on the church, Edward Schillebeeckx argued that the claim that ministry is charismatic does not say anything about the possibility of the control of ministers by the believers or about how the ministers should be elected.[9] His argument was directed against theologians who see charisma as an essentially hierarchical principle. I think Schillebeeckx granted too much to them. I have tried to argue for a stronger thesis: properly understood, a charismatic notion of ministry requires the participation of the local church in the election and ordination of the minister.

Basing his demand for participation of believers in church-political decisions on baptism, Schillebeeckx argued forcefully that at the root of the insistence on exclusion of believers from decision-making in the church lies a 'concealed ideology' according to which the proper church authority is always in the right ('might is right'). Being an insider, Schillebeeckx knows more about ideological elements in Catholic (official) ecclesiology than I do. As an outsider, however, I cannot help but agree with him. But then neither he nor I have addressed, let alone refuted, what I consider to be the strongest of (in my view, unpersuasive!) theological arguments in favour of the essentially hierarchical structure of the church: God, it can be argued as Ratzinger has done in many of his writings, is present in and works through the 'whole' – the 'whole Christ', head and body; but in order to act concretely, the 'whole' requires a concrete 'one' – the one who acts both *in persona ecclesiae* and (therefore?) *in persona Christi*. Augustine's phrase 'the whole Christ' contains a whole ecclesiology (and a good deal of soteriology!). Whether the justification of the hierarchical structures in the church is nothing else but a concealed ideology depends to a large extent on whether the notion of the 'whole Christ' is theologically persuasive.[10]

Notes

1. See John Smyth, *The Works of John Smyth*, ed. W. T. Whitley, Cambridge 1915, 267, 274.

2. For such argumentation see Joseph Ratzinger, *Das neue Volk Gottes. Entwürfe zur Ekklesiologie*, Düsseldorf 1969; Joseph, Cardinal Ratzinger, *Theologische Prinzipienlehre. Bausteine zur Fundamentaltheologie*, Munich 1982.

3. See Miroslav Volk, 'Democracy and the Crisis of the Socialism Project. Toward a Post-Revolutionary Theology of Liberation', *Transformation* 7, 1990, iii, 4,11–16.

4. Joseph Ratzinger, 'Demokratisierung der Kirche?', in Joseph Ratzinger and Hans Maier, *Demokratie in der Kirche. Möglichkeiten, Grenzen, Gefahren*, Werdende Welt 16, Limburg 1970, 9–46: 26f.

5. So recently Norbert Baumert, 'Charisma – Versuch einer Sprachregelung', *Theologie und Philosophie* 66, 1991, 21–48: 32ff.

6. Similarly Wolfhart Pannenberg, *The Church*, Philadelphia 1977, 99–115: 109.

7. Smyth, *Works* (n.1), 256.

8. The inseparability of consecration and election is perceived by Ratzinger ('Demokratisierung' [n.4], 42), though he uses this idea to insist that the whole church (i.e. the pope) has to participate not only in the consecration but also in the election of a bishop.

9. Edward Schillebeeckx, *Church: the Human Story of God*, London and New York 1990.

10. David Cole made valuable suggestions about the style of a previous version of this article.

Indigenous African Churches and the Quest for Democracy

Michel Legrain

Religious communities or families which emerged from missionary Christianity abound in Black Africa. Westerners often denote them by pejorative terms: sects, dissident churches, syncretistic churches, sometimes reserving a capital C for those which in their eyes merit the description of major Churches. With less scorn but still with a good deal of condescension, these Western Christians sometimes use expressions which they feel to be more neutral and non-judgmental: independent or separatist churches, black messianisms. But many African theologians reject all these terms outright, because they put the churches in question outside, or at the periphery of, an ecclesial orthodoxy the criteria and frontiers of which are defined only by the Western churches. That is why the Dominican Sibde Semporé, from Burkina Faso, prefers to speak of Afro-Christian churches, which others call nativist churches, in the sense that they have been founded by Africans and for the benefit of Africans, while continuing to be centred on Christ. Yet others talk rather of indigenous churches, autochthonous churches or new churches.

Always fond of figures and statistics, Westerners estimate that the members of these churches are distributed between 6,000 and 8,000 distinct churches, and form a mobile and progressive mass of between eighteen and twenty million people, about fifteen per cent of all Blacks baptized on this continent. And it is possible that numbers will double by the beginning of the third millennium, which is now so close. However, that is just an estimate, for a baptized individual can claim to belong to one or other of these new churches without renouncing links with his or her original church, which may be Catholic or Protestant.

Among the common denominators among these Afro-Christian churches, two are worth remembering. First, they fundamentally challenge the imposition of religious structures and approaches which came into being elsewhere, and which either get in the way of or alienate the Christian expressions of the Black African populations which have been touched by the grace of Christ. A second characteristic is that these new churches usually come into being around a charismatic leader, a strong personality with little respect for democratic procedures of a Western kind. Having perceived a human and spiritual gap which none of the Christian contributions from overseas had been able to fill, an indigenous prophet has arisen. A phenomenon with irrepressible aspirations draws enthusiastic crowds. This local moving force does not even need to proclaim, 'Let those who love me follow me', since people attach themselves to it as iron filings attach themselves to the magnet. When a prophet appeared in Palestine, whether he was called John the Baptist or Jesus of Nazareth, did he infringe the freedom of those who walked unconstrainedly in his footsteps?

I. Indigenous churches and political and cultural independence

Democracy remains an illusion for a human group as long as that group feels itself to be a minority which is culturally and politically done down by a dominant group which imposes its choices and its laws on it. The bubbling up of nationalistic revivals, which is also taking place in Europe, shows how typical a contemporary situation this is.

Numerous customary African chiefs found the colonial occupation hard to bear. Their authority was either diminished, shifted from its traditional focus, supervised, or eclipsed by the incoming representatives of the colonizing powers.

If it is difficult to deny that some fomentors of rebellion were primarily fired by personal or tribal interests; others, by contrast, put the survival of their clan and its culture in first place. And when these leaders were stamped by the Bible and Christianity, they readily put themselves in the line of the great liberators and prophets of the first covenant. Without rejecting the uniqueness of the basic mediation of Jesus who became the Christ, many of these indigenous prophets saw themselves as special envoys from God to their people, so that the people thought in terms of salvation from a messenger (or messiah) which emerged from this specific portion of humanity.

Obviously the colonial, military, administrative and religious authorities found it difficult to take the success of these new messiahs, who were a danger to the established order. Thus in the Belgian Congo, Simon Kimbangu (1889–1931) was arrested, put on trial and imprisoned for life, a sentence which amounted to thirty years. But the blood of the martyrs is an extraordinary leaven. Recognized in 1959 on the eve of the independence of Zaire, the Church of Jesus Christ on Earth by Simon Kimbangu, better known as the Kimbanguist Church, came to be affiliated to the World Council of Churches in 1969. It claims five million members. We might note in passing that on the advice of American anti-colonialists, when he was still a worker in an oil refinery in Kinshasa, Kimbangu took the religious route, the only one which could put off direct confrontation for a while. On the other side of the great river, in the French Congo, Andre Matswa was condemned to death in 1941. His aims were essentially political, and he would have been the first to be surprised that his followers made him a kind of Black Christ. The same mistake was made over William Wade Harris (1865–1929), born in Liberia and imprisoned for political reasons, who took refuge on the Ivory Coast and was then expelled from there. He preached the renunciation of fetishes and fidelity to the Mosaic law; it is claimed that he baptized more than 100,000 faithful with his own hands. While numerous converts rejoined the great churches, others were able to keep outside the imported church structures and thus founded autonomous indigenous churches, transforming the prophet Harris into a real messiah, and his preaching into a religion with many facets: Harrisism.

Racial segregation also seriously infringed democratic principles. In South Africa, the official policy of apartheid led to an automatic segregation between White Christians and Black or Coloured Christians. Apart from the Catholic and Anglican churches which resisted these measures of strict physical separation between Christians of different churches, the other churches proved conformist. To counter this ostracism which confined them to being socially second-class citizens, the Blacks felt the need to create their own churches. Some of these took the name Ethiopian or Ethiopianist churches, and that is not without significance. On the one hand, for ancient authors as for the biblical redactors the designation 'Ethiopia' was probably a symbol for the whole of Black Africa. On the other hand, the Christians of Ethiopia were able to preserve a marked originality in their church, not only in doctrine but also in liturgy and discipline.

One might have expected that once the much coveted political independence had been achieved, the indigenous religions could have come on happy days. A number of them prospered to such a degree that they became established and set up a hierarchy, like so many of the aging religions. In so doing they sometimes lost a good deal of credibility with the masses, who were again frustrated by the often inappropriate functioning of the apparatuses and values which had been put in place during the period of colonization. On top of this there is increased cultural frustration, since now that external enemies have been removed, people find themselves alone in facing a persistent process of indigenous deculturation.

II. The demands of democracy and religious revivals

Democratic aspirations becomes all the more pressing when a social group becomes aware that it is being seriously held back in its quest for the better life that it envisages. It perceives that the existing political, economic, social and religious order is getting in the way of its own demands for justice, freedom and flourishing. Faced with the triumphant imperialism of Western technologies and the declared superiority of the Christian religion over traditional religions, African societies feel wounded and humiliated.

If the earthen vessel is not to be shattered by the iron vessel, realism requires that those who are driven by a real concern for emancipation should choose a sphere of confrontation and combat which allows some rebalancing of the forces involved. The rise of original religious movements soon proved a powerful lever, dynamic enough to set in train the recapture of an autonomy which had been on the road to failure.

Those who seek to stand up to social and religious structures which they feel to be alienating have no alternative but to resort to the Spirit, that great reducer of chaos. In this respect the Aladura churches are worth attention. Arising in Nigeria after the First World War, the Aladura current, which has now divided into several hundred churches, has flourished principally among the populations in the Gulf of Benin. These Christians became aware that they could enter into communication with the Spirit by themselves becoming great people of prayer (Aladura, in the Yoruba language). This is a prayer with a typically biblical and African stamp, involving song, rhythm and dance, with paroxystic forms like visions, trances, ecstasies and certain phenomena of healing. The African who prays does not take refuge in the lofty chamber of his soul: he does not desert either his personal or his collective body but revitalizes them both, thus making contact with a power and a harmony which had been reduced by evil influences. In this way the conjunctive tissue of society threatened with disintegration is reconstituted. However, this revival of the covenant and common life cannot come about unless individuals confess their sins and undertake their own conversion. And like the people of the Bible or the Qur'an, by taking off their shoes before entering into the ritual of prayer, the worshippers of the Church of Heavenly Christianity, to take one example, signify both their availability to God and their commitment to struggle against all the spheres of evil.

In the African perspective, when the Aladura faithful rediscover health and equilibrium, even where Western medical treatments have failed, it is not by recourse to fetishistic practices, but through a gift of God brought about by the imposition of the hands of brothers and sisters who in this way exercise a real ministry. Here it is more than a matter of recovering a physical function which has been impaired or repairing a broken organ: it is a matter of restoring happy or harmonious relations with those around and with the cosmos, in both their tangible and their intangible dimensions.

According to the apostle Paul (Gal. 5.19–25), the action of the Spirit is manifested when the 'works of the flesh', like libertinism, magic, discord or rebellion, give way to the fruits of the Spirit, like peace, good will, self-control and patience. In practice, aiming at certain results, the collectivity as it prays discovers the secret resources of its own African and Christian identity. Clearly this restores its faith in its liberation and in its dignity.

Surely it is evident that there is a close relationship between these spiritual struggles of the indigenous African churches and the efforts of the Anglo-Saxon revivalist communities of the past or the charismatic brotherhoods of today.

Finally, let us note that because of the very factors which led to its birth, Protestantism has proved more capable of prompting constant religious revivals than Catholicism, since the latter is persuaded that it is by always ploughing the same furrow, now well defined, that it will succeed in proclaiming the good news of Jesus Christ to all the populations of our planet.

III. The indigenous churches, evangelizers of the Catholic Church?

Is such a sub-title mere provocation? None of the great conventional churches welcomes lessons about the gospel, especially from young daughters who are readily accused of being heretics or bastards, whose doctrines are thought to be naively syncretistic and whose morals are thought to be doubtful.

Systematic denegration is common nowadays, not only between rival commercial houses, but even between religions when, laying claim to exclusiveness, they become assertive and dominating.

It would certainly be childish to close one's eyes to some of the ambiguities, inadequacies and errors of the indigenous African churches.

Thus in the name of the spirit of the gospel and of the equal dignity of men and women, it is difficult to rally to those tenets of Harrisism which endorse polygamy. But fairness demands that everyone should not be tarred with the same brush. Thus Kimbanguism favours monogamy: the indissolubility and sacramentality of marriage. However, here again we must not focus on one or another expression of conjugal or family life in a cultural setting, remembering the church fathers, who, over the centuries, dared to ask questions about the best specific ways of helping their flock to live out their sexuality in a way which is closer to the calls of the gospel.

Not without reason, the African peoples denounced the religious imperialism which went with the establishment of the colonial empires of the nineteenth and twentieth centuries. With the certainty of conquerors, they presented the indigenous peoples with a Catholicism the essentials and the details of which had been arrested in the West, and which they had to adopt as they were: from the catechism to liturgical rules, from religious vestments to specific forms to be used if a marriage was to be legitimate. There was a concern to supplant and sweep away local beliefs, which were regarded as dangerous devilries or primitive superstitions. Well before the era of decolonization, a wave of demands swept through the local churches, prompted by different experiences, aimed at greater sensitivity to African cultural sensibilities. But when it was faced with this call, the hierarchy replied by tightening the screws, with the result that many people went elsewhere or vegetated where they were.

Our Catholicism, after a time of hesitation, has given a welcome to the charismatic movements, and this new dialogue, with its demands and its constraints, is certainly proving profitable here and there, bringing out certain riches of the gospel which to some degree are hidden by traditional Catholicism.

On the other hand, one cannot say that the theologies of liberation, even when they are clearly demarcated from Marxism-Leninism, have been able to benefit from the perseverance of a critical audience with a desire to understand.

As for the contributions of the Christian religions which have arisen in Black Africa, there is as yet no concern to study seriously what ensures their undeniable success, even among supposedly committed African Catholics who are thought to be serious. Are these more global approaches on the part of the indigenous African churches really a betrayal of the gospel, on the grounds that they reject our well-established dualistic Western perceptions like body/soul, nature/grace, theology/anthropology, natural religion/revealed religion, earthly happiness/external salvation? Are the indigenous communities less democratic because they do not practise a nominal vote in designating some of their leaders? Is the choice of a religious leader by acclamation less democratic than an authoritarian designation by a remote hierarchy? Is not their self-financing a necessary course and an exemplary lesson for churches which do not want to be colonized by any other church, even spiritually? Does not the interpretation of the Word of God by those who love the Bible sometimes take the gospel route as well as that which is devised by highly educated people or those who are set in authority? And why, finally, persist in describing efforts at inculturation by independent African churches as syncretism, with wholly negative connotations, when the Catholic Church has never used the term syncretism of its borrowings from Jewish, Greek, Roman, Barbarian and Slavonic cultures?

If it wants to be effective, the forthcoming African synod should turn, not so much to the internal problems of the functioning of the Catholic church in Black Africa, as to the reasons for the blockages which prevent Catholicism from inculturating itself deeply among the vast populations of baptized Africans.

As we know, if it is to attain universality, a religion has to transcend all cultures. But can Catholicism detach itself sufficiently from the first cultural cradles in which it developed, in such a way as not to impose on other cultures, over and above the demands of the gospel, the many secondary deposits which have marked its past? We need to dare to deepen the basis of the religious expressions that the Catholic Church forged for itself in the West over the course of the centuries. We need to dare to criticize and relativize, in the light of the gospel, in such a way as to allow other cultural expressions of the same Catholic faith to be born, grow and bear an original fruit. We need to dare to depart from Catholicism as a self-sufficient system, sure of itself on all fronts, in order finally to arrive at a true catholicity. In current theological language that is called inculturation. And it involves constant communal and very delicate work, of a kind that exercises our imaginations over both the call of the gospel and the cultural realities of the peoples who are trying to welcome the good news.

The building of bridges with other cultures, other religions, other wisdoms, can be facilitated by the experiences of the indigenous African churches. They too, like us, can see that in our religious fields the wheat and the tares are mixed. Each church must confess today, in all modesty, that what we are realizing in our present churches is far from representing the extraordinary cultural riches of all our common humanity, called in its totality and its diversity to become the people of God.

Translated by John Bowden

III · Concrete Recommendations

Prospects for a More 'Democratized' Church

James H. Provost

In the light of the diverse meanings of 'democracy' as well as the ecclesiological concerns raised when such political terminology is applied to the church today, one might object that there are no realistic prospects for a more 'democratized' church. The church is a theological reality, not a secular government; its power comes from Christ, not the people; it is served by a hierarchy which governs not on the basis of the consent of the governed, but as the continuation of the apostolic college missioned by Christ.

On the other hand, as is evident from the other articles in this issue, the application to the church of principles often identified with democracy is an idea which continues to attract attention. To explore the prospects for the application of some of these principles to the church, this study proceeds in three stages. First, several fundamental considerations are explored to put such concerns in a better context. Then, as examples of prospects for a more democratized church, the 1983 Code of Canon Law's application of certain key 'democratic' principles within the church will be examined. Finally, it will be important to explore candidly some of the restraints on these prospects.

Context

There are three considerations which set the context for exploring prospects for a more 'democratic' church: the current state of transition in the church as it receives Vatican II, the reasons for the current interest in democracy world-wide and in the church, and the understanding of the church as communion and mission.

1. The church, and even church law, is undergoing a major shift in thinking. Paul VI termed this a *novus habitus mentis*, a new way of thinking, which is characteristic of the Second Vatican Council and which was to characterize the revision of the church's law.[1] One aspect of this new thinking is the shift in understanding of the church from a state-model (perfect society and monarchy, as articulated by Ottaviani and others) to a communion-mission perspective, more theological in its roots and having important repercussions for praxis.

John Paul II identified these repercussions as part of the 'newness' of the Second Vatican Council. In promulgating the Code of Canon Law for the Latin Church he listed these elements of such a new thinking: the church as people of God, hierarchical authority as service, the church as a communion, the participation by all members in the three-fold *munera* of Christ and their common rights and obligations related to this, and the church's commitment to ecumenism.[2] In addition to providing the basis for understanding the new canon law, these elements set an agenda for the church, an agenda which might be considered to form the basis for a kind of 'democratizing' of the church.

We address this agenda at a time of transition in the church. We are in the midst of the reception of Vatican II, a process which will take at least three generations, and a process which is already pointing up the compromises which are the glory but also the weaknesses of the conciliar documents. This is a *kairos*, a crucial time in which we can grasp the deeper meaning of the conciliar insights; but it is also a moment which, if lost, may make it extremely difficult to recapture those insights in the future.

This is also a time of transition in the relationship of the church and the world. Not only is the church's own understanding of this relationship in transition, but the 'world' itself is in a state of major transformation. Political, social, cultural and religious forces are no longer cleanly aligned, and the realignment which we can expect to take place in this decade poses as major a challenge to the church as it does to other international institutions. This is added reason to take the present opportunities seriously, and to address the agenda set before the church by the Council and reaffirmed in the promulgation of the Latin Code.

2. A second major element of the present context is located in the current interest in democracy. Not only is it on the lips of everyone – North, South, East and West; it is also figuring importantly in current documents of the church's *magisterium*.[3] But this is not enough to explain its recurrent interest as a concept which may be applicable within the church. There is something more specific to the Catholic experience which needs to be acknowledged.

A parallel may help to identify this added factor. In recent years it has been suggested that the principle of subsidiarity – a principle of Catholic social teaching – should be applied within the church. Reviewing these developments, Joseph Komonchak argues that 'subsidiarity' is a heuristic principle developed to counter the growing centralization of state-authority, and that its application within the church has been proposed to counter 'practical developments which were restricting rightful claims to freedom and self-responsibility'.[4] It could be that appeals to democracy within the church arise from the same concerns and seek a similar result.

Appeals to democracy are often heard in response to what are perceived as autocratic uses of power, whether by parish pastors who on their own cancel popular programmes, or by Roman authorities who insist on their prerogative to name bishops with no apparent consideration for the local pastoral situation. Suggestions that more democracy might help the church are heard when the Roman Curia is perceived as attempting to 'micromanage' (i.e., control down to the most minute detail) the entire church, when national or diocesan church bureaucracies appear isolated from local realities, when pastoral councils are ignored or dissolved. In other words, 'democracy' is frequently presented as the solution to feelings of marginalization, over-centralization, or pastoral ineptitude.

But as Komonchak noted for subsidiarity, so too for those issues which occasion the appeal to democracy within the church, these problems need 'to be addressed in the broad context not only of the powerful centralizing tendencies of the last two centuries but also of the social theory, imported from without, which legitimated them'.[5] When the claim is made that the 'church is not a democracy', this is often heard as a claim that the church is an autocracy or monarchy. Such were the social theories that buttressed the style of authority which has come to be perceived as typical of the Catholic Church.

People are familiar with democracy from daily life, even if the 'democracies' with which they are familiar vary considerably. Although democracy is no panacea for tensions in the church, any more than it is a perfect solution for social and political life, it is nevertheless a style of relating in human society for which people have definite expectations, and one which influences Catholics as well as others in the body politic. It is not surprising, then, that democratic elements are seen as a way to counter-balance excesses left over from a previous way of understanding the church, excesses which continue to haunt Catholic life.

3. Emerging from Vatican II have been two perceptions of the church which have been embraced as articulating the nature of the church creatively, dynamically. These are that the church is a communion, and

that it is mission. Putting aside ideological uses which may have been made of these concepts, it is clear from papal and episcopal statements, as well as the writings of theologians, that these concepts do provide important insights into who we are as a church, and therefore how we should be acting.

Communion and mission both have deep theological roots, participating each in its own way in our understanding of who God is (a communion of three persons, who reveal themselves to us through their missions), of who Christ is (the hypostatic union, one who is sent on a mission), and of the continued working of God in our midst (we are drawn into the communion of trinitarian life by grace, and as a church we continue the mission of Christ in teaching, sanctifying and bringing about God's reign).

But they also have operational dimensions. Communion is expressed in hospitality, in being 'at home' anywhere in the church, in bonds of mutual aid and support, in prayer and service for the members of the communion. It is articulated in a special manner at the Eucharist, where in Holy Communion we share divine life with one another. The celebrations of the Eucharist are linked through the hierarchical communion of those who preside at the altar and in the church.

Mission is expressed in preaching the gospel, celebrating the sacraments, and acting on behalf of justice; that is, in taking those practical steps needed to continue Christ's mission. The transformation of the world in preparation for God's reign includes evangelizing those who have not yet heard the gospel, deepening the faith of those who have, and working to bring about that unity of Christ's disciples through which the world will come to believe.

Communion and mission are not products of democratic theory, nor are they explicitly 'democratic'. Yet they both rely upon certain key considerations which are also central to democratic principles: a fundamental equality of all in the communion, participation by all in the mission, an informed community, public expression of opinions, etc. It is to the expression of some of these democratic principles in the current Code of Canon Law that we now turn.

Democratic principles in church law

The church's law does not use the term 'democracy'. It does, however, echo the teaching of the Council and of recent popes in placing considerable emphasis on co-responsibility. It is here that a number of democratic principles are evident. For example, shared responsibility is rooted in the fundamental equality of all believers in their dignity as

Christians in communion, and in their responsibility to participate in the mission of the church (c. 208). By baptism, all the Christian faithful are sharers in Christ's priestly, prophetic and royal office in their own way, and 'are called to exercise the mission God has entrusted to the Church to fulfill in the world' (c. 204, §1). All are responsible 'to promote the growth of the Church and its continual sanctification' (c. 210). 'All the Christian faithful have the duty and the right to work so that the divine message of salvation may increasingly reach the whole of humankind in every age and in every land' (c. 211).

This fundamental equality in the church as communion and mission establishes a foundation for increased application of various democratic principles. John Paul II identifies several such principles; participation in making choices which affect the life of the community, a role in the selection of leaders, provision for the accountability of leaders, and structures for effective participation and shared responsibility.[6]

1. Decision-making. Making decisions is a complex process involving the gathering of information, identification of options, making choices, and seeing to the implementation of decisions once they are made. Access to information and the possibility of free expression of opinions are central to democratic decision-making.[7] They are also central to the first three stages of the decision-making process in the church.

(*a*) The Code is less explicit than the church's social teaching in regard to the right to information within the church. Pastoral instructions from the Pontifical Council for Social Communications have highlighted 'the fundamental right of dialogue and information within the Church' and the necessity 'to continue to seek effective means, including a responsible use of media of social communications, for realizing and protecting this right'.[8] The canons refer to information mainly in terms of what the Christian faithful express to church authorities: petitioning to have their needs attended to (c. 212, §2), and expressing their opinions on matters which pertain to the good of the church (c. 212, §3). There is little about the freedom of information in the church, or about the responsibility of the authorities to inform the rest of the faithful about the condition of the church or even the needs of the apostolate. The only public reporting the law requires is a public financial accounting to the faithful concerning the goods they have offered to the church (c. 1287, §2).

The expression of public opinion in the church is couched in very cautious terms: 'in accord with the knowledge, competence and preeminence which they possess', Christians 'have the right and even at times a duty to manifest to the sacred pastors their opinion on matters which pertain to the good of the Church'. Only after informing church officials, and so long as they take 'due regard for the integrity of faith and morals and reverence toward their pastors, and with consideration for the common good and the dignity of persons', are the faithful recognized to 'have the right to make their opinion known to the other Christian faithful' (c. 212, §3). The cautions, however, must not empty this right of all practical meaning, for it is indeed an expression of the 'fundamental right to dialogue and information' on which the Vatican insists.[9]

(b) Church law structures formal communication in terms of 'consultation'. The importance of such consultation is reinforced in the present Code, even though its application is still somewhat restricted. At times a superior cannot act validly without consulting a group or certain specified individuals. At other times, the superior must obtain the consent of a group or individuals in order to act (c. 127). This has an evident impact especially in the financial dimension of church life, where a bishop's financial decisions can be subject to advice, consent, or even a veto by an appointed body which could include lay women and men, the finance council.[10] Consultation is also mandated for certain key decisions affecting the pastoral organization of a diocese and in various personnel situations.[11]

In addition to these limit situations (where consultation is required before an action can be valid), the law encourages consultation through a variety of structures. Vatican II called for the church to set up structures through which people could express their views (*Lumen Gentium*, 37), and encouraged at least one such structure, the pastoral council, for each diocese (*Christus Dominus*, 27). The Code has not mandated pastoral councils, but does provide for their possibility in the diocese (c. 511) and in parishes, where they can even be mandated by the bishop after consulting with the presbyteral council (c. 536).[12] These bodies have a special role in pastoral planning, which church documents take seriously and anticipate bishops will do likewise.[13]

In other cases, the Code expands the involvement of the community in various traditional decision-making structures, especially the diocesan synod and particular councils. Participation in diocesan synods and on particular councils has been enlarged to include a variety of people, lay persons as well as clergy and religious. Decisions which are made in these contexts take place in a setting which guarantees open expression of opinion (cc. 443, 463, 465). An application of this same principle is being urged on a continental basis for the special African Synod now under preparation.[14]

(c) The church's law anticipates a broad range of individuals and groups being involved in carrying out the mission, whether internal to the church's own life or in relationship to the world. Church offices are no longer restricted to clergy (c. 228, §1). Although the theoretical foundations are still debated, in practice increasing numbers of lay persons are being involved in the executive functions of church government. Whether motivated by a shortage of clergy or a sensitivity to the fundamental equality of all in the church, the end-result carries certain overtones of democratic participation in community life.

Moreover, the initiative for carrying out decisions is no longer the exclusive domain of church officials. The law recognizes the liberty of all Christians within the church communion to form associations and to assemble (c. 215), two basic liberties in a democratic system. Personal initiative, highly prized in a democracy, is safeguarded as a right in regard to apostolic works, that is, in works which implement the church's mission (c. 216).

2. *Selection of leaders*. Decision-making in the church is highly influenced by who makes the decisions. John Paul II identifies as a democratic principle a role in the selection of a community's leaders. In associations of the faithful and in various other groups in the church the selection process is usually in the hands of the members, but for most official positions the selections are made by members of a clerical hierarchy. This is not inherently anti-democratic if one takes into account the complex nature of a selection process in which the requirements for a specific office should be clarified, qualified candidates must be identified, a choice is made among qualified candidates, and the office is conferred upon that person. The law provides for several systems for these various steps (cf. c. 147). Even where a church official makes the final selection and confers the office, consultation should precede and inform the identification of candidates, and concern for the common good – or as the final canon puts it, concern for the salvation of souls (c. 1752) – should direct the making of the final choice.

Moreover, the selection of church leaders by election has a long standing within the canonical tradition and is still residually present in the current law.[15] Even within the hierarchical structure of the church, some officials are elected by an electoral college.[16] Elections, however, have been so restricted over the centuries that consultation, rather than direct election, provides the most realistic channel for increasing the participation of the whole church in the selection of its leaders. The norms for selecting bishops and parish pastors, persons with special importance in directing the life of the church communion and in its mission, call for some consultation within the community.[17] It must be noted, however, that in both cases the requirement to consult is expressed in very cautious terms and is not for the validity of the appointment; only in reference to the finance officer is consultation required for a valid appointment to a diocesan office (c. 494).

There is a tendency in the church to restrict or ignore existing structures of consultation in the selection of bishops, whether these are chapters of canons with their ancient prerogatives, or more recently established consultative bodies who, under existing norms, cannot be consulted as a body. Indeed, with some episcopal appointments in recent years, observers have wondered whether anyone in touch with the local pastoral (or even financial!) situation was listened to in the selection process.

The criteria for the selection of church officials is supposed to be spelled out in the law (c. 149). Those for bishops and parish pastors, for example, are given in the Code (cc. 387 and 521). Such open identification of the qualifications is in keeping with accepted practices in a democratic system. But in practice, observers have noted that at least for bishops, appointments seem to be based on other criteria, not stated in the law but clearly evident in the questionnaires circulated to ascertain a candidate's views.[18]

3. Accountability. Accountability remains one of the weak spots in the Church's legal system. Theoretically the hierarchical structure provides for vertical accountability, with parish and diocesan offices accountable to the diocesan bishop, and with the bishop accountable to the Apostolic See. In practice, the system is proving too complex for effective accountability. Interventions tend to be in terms of crisis rather than a systematic review of missions, plans, and actual performance.

Although the pope is not an absolute ruler, but must respect the limits of divine law, revelation, the church's tradition and *magisterium*, and other elements too numerous even for a conciliar commission to mention during Vatican II,[19] there is no one to whom he is accountable within the church (cc. 333, §3 and 1404). There is no structured system of accountability for higher officials of Roman dicasteries. Episcopal conferences are accountable to their members, but since the conferences are the members, this is not an especially effective means of accountability. Yet the life of the community is clearly affected by the decisions, actions or omissions of the pope, the curia, or bishops' conferences.

The prospects for a more 'democratized' church may seem to have reached their ultimate limit here, for without the possibility of holding leaders accountable, how can there be any assurance that participation by members of the church will be taken seriously, or that officials will indeed be attentive to the common good, to the salvation of souls?

The church has had to struggle with this issue from the time of Paul's confrontation with Peter over the treatment of Gentile converts (Gal. 2.11–14). This kind of remonstration to supreme authority has enjoyed a long and at times effective use in the church.[20] Moreover, one of the reasons for the extreme caution with which the right to express public opinion is articulated in the Code is that public opinion does in fact have considerable weight in the church, even while church officials may deny this in principle. It is also true that not all so-called democratic systems provide for direct recall of officials by the members of the community.

Ultimately, as a religious body rooted in spiritual commitment and seeking to live by supernatural values, the greatest accountability still resides in conscience. But in limit situations, while the church law may be weak or silent, in practice the means are usually found to redress the problem. This is perhaps one of the areas most in need of reflection and development in present church order, but also one in which democratic principles may provide insights to assist in the canonical development.[21]

Restraints on prospects

There are many constraints on the prospects for a more 'democratized' church; only three will be discussed here, and these only briefly. These are the lack of adequate protection for rights in the church, a developing attitude of alienation among Catholics with regard to church structures, and a lack of consensus concerning mission within the church.

1. While the codes of canon law for Eastern Churches and for the Latin Church proclaim a list of rights and duties common to all the faithful, and special lists for laity, clergy, and religious, the law does not provide effective means to vindicate these rights. Without adequate protection, rights may be high ideals but they have little practical consequence.

Church courts are currently forbidden to accept cases for the vindication of rights if the controversy arises from an act of administrative power (c. 1400, §2). Private opinions circulated by the Apostolic Signatura, the highest supervisory body for church courts, have held that actions by pastors, by lay school administrators, and by religious superiors are all covered by this prohibition. The most common causes for seeking to vindicate rights, however, arise from acts or omissions by those with administrative power. To limit relief in these cases to non-existent administrative tribunals or to recourse to hierarchical authorities, is for many people to deny them relief at all. The effort is too great, the distance to the authorities is too vast, and the cost is beyond the resources of many people.

Without an effective means to vindicate rights, there can be little hope for a more 'democratized' church in any realistic terms. But this is not just a question of 'democracy'; it is a concern for justice, and therefore one which the church which proclaims justice cannot ignore.[22]

2. The alienation of Catholics from church structures has been observed for some time. There seem to be at least two factors at work. One is the increasing privatization of religion, in which people are separating their public lives and their religious practice; the other factor is the disillusionment of many practising Catholics with the tensions and struggles which have marked the relations between so-called 'traditional' and so-called 'liberal' Catholics since Vatican II.

The restraint this poses to a more 'democratized' church is similar to the danger a loss in political interest poses to a democratic state. If the members no longer take an active role in the life of the group, then democratic principles will not work in practice. If people are uninterested, and so do not participate in consultation, in building the life of the community, or in carrying out the church's mission, the results are tragic far beyond the question of 'democracy' in the church. The results touch the very heart of the church itself, something about which church officials and members cannot remain indifferent.

3. Perhaps one of the most debilitating restraints is the lack of consensus on the church as mission. This may be another result of the privatization of religion and the alienation of people from church structures, but it also affects those deeply involved in the life of the church. The post-Vatican II period has been marked by concern with structures and the inner life of the church. At the same time, a sense of mission, of having a message which is good news for the societies in which Catholics live and for people everywhere, has diminished. Some of this is further weakened by disputes over loyalty to non-infallible teachings, by evident mistrust toward local church leaders (hence, the demand for an oath of fidelity), and by an uncertainty of how to proclaim the good news while at the same time respecting the ecumenical and inter-religious values the church has so recently recognized.

Efforts by the pope and various leaders of movements to galvanize Catholics into a more evangelistic mood are not receiving an immediate, positive response. The reasons are many, but the end result restrains the development of a more 'democratized' church in several ways. Those who issue the call to mission, in the hope of creating a more positive response, appear intent on a more centralized approach to the whole mission endeavour. Those who for various reasons find the appeals unconvincing seem reluctant to engage in a process to create a more workable consensus on mission. Ultimately, it is the mission which suffers, and with it the very reality of being church. Democracy is not a panacea to energize the community, but respect for democratic principles may be one manner of relating more dynamically to the lived experience and expectations of many Catholics, and could contribute toward the development of a more effective consensus.

Prospects for a more 'democratized' church are not so bleak as they may have seemed at the outset. There are a number of factors within the church's own law which, if addressed competently and consistently, will indeed foster the application of democratic principles within the Catholic Church. But the restraints on these possibilities must also be candidly acknowledged and courageously addressed.

Notes

1. Paul VI, allocution of 20 November 1965, *Communicationes* 1, 1969, 38–42.

2. John Paul II, apostolic constitution *Sacrae disciplinae leges*, 25 January 1983, *AAS* 75/2, 1983, xii.

3. For example, *Gaudium et Spes*, no. 75; Paul VI, letter *Octogesima adveniens*, no. 47; John Paul II, encyclical *Sollicitudo rei socialis*, 30 December 1987, no. 44; id., encyclical *Centesimus annus*, 1 May 1991, no. 46.

4. Joseph A. Komonchak, 'Subsidiarity in the Church: The State of the Question', in *The Nature and Future of Episcopal Conferences*, ed. Hervé Legrand, Julio Manzanares and Antonio García y García, Washington DC 1988, 343.

5. Ibid.

6. *Centesimus annusn*, no. 46: 'The Church values the democratic system inasmuch as it ensures the participation of citizens in making political choices, guarantees to the governed the possibilities both of electing and holding accountable those who govern them, and of replacing them through peaceful means when appropriate. . . . Authentic democracy . . . requires . . . structures of participation and shared responsibility.'

7. See the discussion in Antonio Osuna Fernández-Largo, 'La Democratizacion de la Iglesia. Recelos y pretensiones', *Razón y Fe* 220, 1989, 53–65.

8. Pontifical Council for Social Communications, *Communio et progressio*, 23 May 1971, nos. 114–121; id., *Aetatis novae*, 17 March 1992, no. 10.

9. *Aetatis novae*, no. 10.

10. Cf. c. 492. This group supervises the financial activity in a diocese; it must annually prepare a diocesan budget and a diocesan financial report (c. 493), and is to examine the annual reports of non-exempt administrators in the diocese (1287, §1). Its advice must be sought in the hiring and firing of the diocesan finance officer, and the finance officer reports to the council on his activities (c. 494). The bishops must consult the finance council before imposing taxes (c. 1263), before doing more important acts of administration (c. 1277) or setting standards for these which apply to entities subject to the bishop (c. 1281, §2), before approving investments of endowments (c. 1305), and before reducing burdens imposed in executing wills for pious causes (c. 1310, §2).

Its consent must be obtained before the bishop can perform acts of extraordinary administration (c. 1277) or authorize alienation of church property over a minimum set by the bishops' conference (c. 1292, §1).

11. There are several situations in which the presbyteral council must be consulted: cc. 461, §1 (whether to hold a diocesan synod); 515, §2 (erect or modify parishes); 531 (use of offerings to parish for sacramental services); 536 (to require parish pastoral councils); 1215, §2 and 1222, §2 (starting or closing churches); 1263 (diocesan taxes); 1742, §1 (list of pastors for personnel actions). In financial matters frequently the college of consultors is to be consulted in addition to finance council.

Experts must be consulted when specialized knowledge is required; e.g., to declare an irregularity to receive orders or to lift an impediment to the exercise of orders, when these are due to psychic problems (cc. 1041, 1°; 1044, §2, 2°); to alienate property (c. 1293, §1, 2°); in judicial trials (c. 1574); etc.

12. The code does mandate a finance council in every diocese and parish (cc. 492 and 537); some might wonder if this expresses a priority of finances over pastoral concerns in the law.

13. See, for example, the Congregation for Bishops, *Directorium de Pastorali Ministerio Episcoporum*, 22 February 1973, nos. 148–152; *Aetatis novae*, nos. 20–33.

14. See IMBISA Seminar, 'Practical Proposals', 26 October 1991: *Catholic International* 3/9, 1–14 May 1992, 418.

15. See cc. 147, 164–179.

16. The pope is elected by the cardinals under eighty years of age (cf. c 332, §1). When a diocese becomes vacant, the diocesan administrator is elected by the college of consultors of that diocese (c. 421). These examples are few, but they serve as reminders that centralized selection is not the only acceptable process under church law and need not remain indefinitely as the only means for naming bishops or parish pastors.

17. The papal representative is to consult people in a diocese which is vacant before submitting a list of candidates for diocesan bishop (c. 377, §2), and the diocesan bishop is to consult in order to determine a priest's suitability to pastor a specific parish before appointing a parish pastor (c. 524).

18. See Thomas J. Reese, 'The Selection of Bishops', *America*, 25 August 1984, 65–72, with the text of the questionnaire on p. 69.

19. *Acta Synodalia Sacrosancti Concilii Oecumenici Vaticani II*, Vatican City 1973, 3/1: 247.

20. If a bishop feels aggrieved by a law the pope issues, the bishop can present a *remonstratio* to the pope, which suspends the effect of the law in question until the pope makes a further determination (either enforcing the original law, modifying it, repealing it, or making an exception to it). See Vernz-Vidal, *Ius Canonicum 1: Normae Generales*, Rome 1952, 190–1.

21. Insights from various political systems have aided the church historically in developing its inner structures and procedures. There is no theoretical reason why this analogical use of secular principles has to cease when secular political systems become more democratic.

22. The 1971 Synod of Bishops was especially strong on this point; see 1971 Synod, declaration *De Iustitia in Mundo*, 30 November 1971, III: *AAS* 63, 1971, 933; 1974 Synod, declaration, 25 October 1974, 12, in *Leges Ecclesiae post Codicem iuris canonici editae*, ed. Xaverius Ochoa, 5, Rome 1980, col. 6862.

Contributors

KURT TUDYKA studied constitutional and political science at universities in Germany and the USA. Since 1972 he has been Ordinarius Professor of Political Science at the Catholic University of Nijmegen, The Netherlands. His publications include: *Was ist Demokratie?*, 1969; *Gesellschaftliche Interessen und Auswärtige Beziehungen*, 1969; *Internationale Beziehungen*, 1971; *Kritische Politikwissenschaft*, 1973; *Marktplatz Europa*, 1975; *Multinationale Konzerne*, 1977; *Illusionärer Internationalismus*, 1977; *Macht ohne Grenzen und grenzenlose Ohnmacht*, 1978; *Conflicthaarden in de Derde Wereld*, 1984; *Unions and Employers' Associations*, 1984; *Problems of International Planning*, 1985; *Crisis Situation for Multinational Corporation Trade Unions Councils*, 1987; *Friedenforschung*, 1988; *Radikalismus*, 1988; *Protestbewegung*, 1988; *Weltgesellschaft*, 1989; *Politische Ökonomie*, 1990.
   Address: PO Box 9108 NL, 6500 HK Nijmegen, The Netherlands.

GIUSEPPE ALBERIGO was born in 1926 in Varese, and since 1976 has been Professor of Church History in the Faculty of Political Sciences of the University of Bologna. He is also Secretary of the Institute for Religious Sciences of Bologna. His publications include: *I vescovi italiani al concilio di Trento*, 1959; *Lo sviluppo della dottrina sui poteri nella chiesa universale*, 1964; *Cardinalato e collegialità*, 1969; *Chiesa conciliare*, 1981; *Giovanni XXIII. Profezia nella fedeltà*, 1978; *La Chiesa nella Storia*, 1989, and *Nostalgie di unità*, 1989. He has also written and edited a number of studies on Vatican II and has contributed to many historical and theological journals. He is editor of the journal *Cristianesimo nella Storia* and a member of the Board of Directors of *Concilium*.
   Address: Via G. Mazzini 82, I–40. 138 Bologna, Italy.

WILLY OBRIST studied philosophy and history, and later medicine. After many years working as a specialist on internal medicine, he studied depth psychology and trained to be an analyst. Since 1970 he has been lecturer in the theory of depth psychology at the C. G. Jung Institute in Zurich and has worked at the Stiftung für humanwissenschaftliche Grundlagen-forschung. His research is concerned with the evolution of consciousness. His publications include *Die Mutation des Bewusstseins. Vom archäischen zum heutigen Selbst- und Weltverständnis*, Bern 1980, ²1988; *Neues Bewusstsein und Religiösitat*, Olten 1988; *Archetypen. Natur- und Kulturwissenschaften bestätigen C. G. Jung*, Olten 1990.

Address: St Niklausenstrasse 23, CH-6005 Luzern, Switzerland.

GEOFFREY KING was born in Sydney, Australia, in 1943. He entered the Society of Jesus in 1960, and subsequently gained an honours degree in History from the University of Melbourne (1968) and a doctorate in Canon Law from the Catholic University of America (1979). From 1979 to 1989 he taught Canon Law and Church History in the United Faculty of Theology, Melbourne, and he is currently Director of the East Asian Pastoral Institute, Manila, Philippines, and Moderator of the Executive Committee of the Catholic Biblical Federation. He has published articles on canonical and ecclesiological topics in the *Jurist, Pacifica* and the *East Asian Pastoral Review*.

Address: East Asian Pastoral Institute, PO Box 221, 1101 UP Campus, QC, Philippines.

PETER HUIZING was born in 1911 in Haarlem, The Netherlands. He studied law at the universities of Amsterdam and Nijmegen, philosophy and theology at the Jesuit faculties in Nijmegen and Maastricht, and canon law at the Catholic University of Louvain and the Gregorian University in Rome. He taught at the Jesuit faculty in Maastricht, the canon law faculty at the Gregorian University and Louvain, at the theological faculties at Nijmegen and Tilburg, and in the department of canon law of the Catholic University of America in Washington. His articles have appeared in a variety of scholarly journals.

Address: Berchmanianum, Postbus 9017, 6500 GV Nijmegen, Netherlands.

PATRICIA WALTER, OP, is an assistant professor of systematic theology at St Mary Seminary in Cleveland, Ohio. She has an STL from the Jesuit School of Theology in Berkeley and received her PhD from Graduate Theological Union in Berkeley. She has written on the topics of religious life and ecclesial authority. A member of the Sisters of St Dominic of Adrian, Michigan, she was recently elected Prioress of the Congregation.

Address: Center for Pastoral Leadership, 28700 Euclid, Wickliffe, OH 44092-2527, USA.

GEORGE NEDUNGATT was born in Kerala, India in 1932; he is a member of the Syro-Malabar Church. He entered the Society of Jesus in 1950 and gained licentiates in philosophy and theology in India and a doctorate in canon law from the Pontifical Oriental Institute, Rome, where he has been professor since 1973. From 1981–7 he was dean of the faculty and from 1973–1990 Consultor of the Pontifical Commission for the Revision of the Oriental Code. Since 1991 he has been Consultor of the Pontifical Council for the Interpretation of Legal Texts; he is also editor of *Kanonika*, a new series of publications launched in 1992 by the Faculty of Canon Law of the Oriental Institute covering commentaries and sources of the Oriental Code. His books include *The Covenanters of the Early Syriac-Speaking Church*, Rome 1973, and he has published articles in *The Jurist, Kanon, Nuntia, Orientalia Christiana Periodica, Studia Canonica and Vidyajyoti Journal*.

Address: Pontifical Oriental Institute, Piazza S. Maria Maggiore 7, 00185 Rome, Italy.

BERNARD FRANCK was born in 1930 in German-speaking Lorraine and ordained priest in the diocese of Metz in 1955. After several years of parish work he studied at Strasbourg and in Rome. From 1960–1962 he studied at the Pontifical Ecclesiastical Academy in Rome and from 1962–1968 was in the service of the Vatican Secretariat of State. Since 1968 he has been working in his home diocese. He is a doctor of theology and of canon law. In addition to a number of articles on ecclesiastical jurisprudence and the history of Christian institutions, published mainly in *L'Année Canonique*, Paris, and *Revue de Droit Canonique*, Strasbourg, he has written three books: *Actualité nouvelle des Synodes*, Paris 1980; *Famille, mariage, sexualité dans une perspective chrétienne*, Paris 1980; and *Vers un nouveau droit canonique?*, Paris 1983. He is particularly interested in the pastoral problems of the German-speaking countries and in the sects, new religious movements and New Age movements (on which he is currently writing).

Address: Evêché, PB 690, 57019 Metz Cedex 1, France.

BERMA KLEIN GOLDEWIJK was born in the Netherlands in 1956 and gained a doctorate in theology at the Catholic University of Nijmegen on the ecclesiology of Leonardo Boff. She was chief organizer of the congress on Liberation Theology in Western Europe and with J. van Nieuwenhove wrote a book on it, *Popular Religion, Liberation and Contextual Theology*, 1991. She has also written articles in a variety of journals. Her post-

doctoral work is on Afro-Brazilian religions in the perspective of liberation theology.
Address: Mesdagstraat 18, 6521 MP Nijmegen, The Netherlands.

GREGORY BAUM was born in Berlin in 1923; since 1940 he has lived in Canada. He studied at McMaster University, Hamilton; Ohio State University; the University of Fribourg and the New School for Social Research, New York. He is now Professor of Theology and Social Ethics at McGill University, Montreal. He is editor of *The Ecumenist*; his books include *Religion and Alienation* (1975), *The Social Imperative* (1978), *Catholics and Canadian Socialism* (1980), *The Priority of Labor* (1982), *Ethics and Economics* (1984), and *Theology and Society* (1987).
Address: McGill University, 3520 University St, Montreal H3A 2A7.

MIROSLAV VOLF is Associate Professor of Systematic Theology at Fuller Theological Seminary, Pasadena, California and teaches theology and ethics at Evangelical Theological Faculty, Osijek, Yugoslavia. He was born in Yugoslavia in 1956 and studied theology and philosophy in his native country, in the United States and Germany. He holds a doctorate in theology from the Evangelical-Theological Faculty in Tübingen. Until recently he was the editor of and a regular contributor to a Croatian Christian monthly, *Izvori*. He has published numerous scholarly articles, mainly on political and economic theology and ecclesiology. His books include *Zukunft der Arbeit – Arbeit der Zukunft. Der Arbeitsbegriff bei Karl Marx und seine theologische Wertung*, Munich and Mainz 1988; *Work in the Spirit. Toward a Theology of Work*, New York 1991. He is a member of the Evangelical Church of Yugoslavia.
Address: Evangelisch-Theologisches Seminar, Liebermeisterstrasse 12, D-74 Tübingen, Germany.

MICHEL LEGRAIN, a member of the Missionary Congregation of the Pères du Saint-Esprit, at present divides his time between teaching canon law at the Institut Catholique in Paris, sessions and lectures on questions of sexuality and marriage, and a varied theological ministry for the churches of Africa. Recent works include *Le corps humain*, Paris 1978; *Questions autour du mariage*, Mulhouse 1983; *Aujourd'hui le mariage?*, Paris 1988: *Les divorcés remariés*, Paris 1987; *Remariage et communautés chrétiennes*, Mulhouse 1991, and *Les chrétiens face au divorce*, Paris 1991.
Address: 24 rue Cassette, 75006 Paris, France.

JAMES H. PROVOST is a priest of the diocese of Helena, Montana, and a professor of canon law at The Catholic University of America, where he also chairs the Department of Canon Law. He was born in 1939 and was ordained at the American College in Louvain, Belgium in 1963, after completing theological studies at the University of Louvain. In 1967 he received a doctorate in canon law at the Lateran University in Rome. He serves as the managing editor of *The Jurist*. In addition, from 1980 to 1986 he served as executive coordinator of the Canon Law Society of America. He is one of the directors for the Church Order section of *Concilium*.

Address: Dept of Canon Law, Catholic University of America, Washington, DC 20064, USA.

Members of the Advisory Committee for Ecclesiastical Institutions

Directors

James Provost	Washington DC	United States
Knut Walf	Nijmegen	The Netherlands

Members

John Barry	Edinburgh	Scotland
William Bassett	San Francisco	United States
Jean Bernhard	Strasbourg	France
Michael Breydy	Witten, Ruhr	Germany
Giovanni Cereti	Rome	Italy
James Coriden	Silver Spring Md	United States
Albertus Eysink	Huissen	The Netherlands
Antonio Garcia y Garcia	Salamanca	Spain
Jean Gaudemet	Paris	France
Thomas Green	Washington DC	United States
Joseph Hajjar	Damascus	Syria
Peter Huizing SJ	Nijmegen	The Netherlands
Ruud Huysmans	Voorburg	The Netherlands
Teodoro Jiménez Urresti	Toledo	Spain
Michel Legrain	Paris	France
Julio Manzanares	Salamanca	Spain
Elizabeth McDonough OP	Washington DC	United States
Francis Morrissey OMI	Ottawa	Canada
Hubert Müller	Bonn	Germany
Jean Passicos	Paris	France
Reinhold Sebott SJ	Frankfurt am Main	Germany
Remigiusz Sobański SJ	Warsaw	Poland
Robert Soullard OP	Brussels	Belgium
Luis Vela Sanchez SJ	Madrid	Spain
Francesco Zanchini	Rome	Italy

DATE DUE

HIGHSMITH 45-220